QUICK AND EASY WEEKEND WOODWORKING PROJECTS

EDITORS OF POPULAR WOODWORKING

POPULAR WOODWORKING BOOKS
CINCINNATI, OHIO
www.popularwoodworking.com

READ THIS IMPORTANT SAFETY NOTICE

To prevent accidents, keep safety in mind while you work. Use the safety guards installed on power equipment; they are for your protection. When working on power equipment, keep fingers away from saw blades, wear safety goggles to prevent injuries from flying wood chips and sawdust, wear headphones to protect your hearing, and consider installing a dust vacuum to reduce the amount of airborne sawdust in your woodshop. Don't wear loose clothing, such as neckties or shirts with loose sleeves, or jewelry, such as rings, necklaces or bracelets, when working on power equipment. Tie back long hair to prevent it from getting caught in your equipment. People who are sensitive to certain chemicals should check the chemical content of any product before using it. The authors and editors who compiled this book have tried to make the contents as accurate and correct as possible. Plans, illustrations, photographs and text have been carefully checked. All instructions, plans and projects should be carefully read, studied and understood before beginning construction. In some photos, power tool guards have been removed to more clearly show the operation being demonstrated. Always use all safety guards and attachments that come with your power tools. Due to the variability of local conditions, construction materials, skill levels, etc., neither the editors nor Popular Woodworking Books assumes any responsibility for any accidents, injuries, damages or other losses incurred resulting from the material presented in this book. Prices listed for supplies and equipment were current at the time of publication and are subject to change. Glass shelving should have all edges polished and must be tempered. Untempered glass shelves may shatter and can cause serious bodily injury. Tempered shelves are very strong and if they break will just crumble, minimizing personal injury.

Quick and Easy Weekend Woodworking Projects. Copyright © 2005 by the Editors of Popular Woodworking. Printed and bound in China. All rights reserved. No part of this book may be reproduced in any form or by any electronic or mechanical means, including information storage and retrieval systems, without permission in writing from the publisher, except by a reviewer, who may quote brief passages in a review. Published by Popular Woodworking Books, an imprint of F+W Publications, Inc., 4700 East Galbraith Road, Cincinnati, Ohio, 45236. First edition.

Visit our Web site at www.popularwoodworking.com for information on more resources for woodworkers.

Other fine Popular Woodworking Books are available from your local bookstore or direct from the publisher.

09   08   07   06   05   5   4   3   2   1

Library of Congress Cataloging-in-Publication Data

Quick and easy weekend woodworking projects / from the editors of Popular woodworking.
   p.   cm.
   Includes index.
   ISBN 1-55870-746-8 (alk. paper)
   1. Woodwork--Patterns.   I. Title: Quick and easy weekend woodworking projects.
II. Popular woodworking.
TT180.Q52 2005
684'.08--dc22   2004057649

EDITORS: Amy Hattersley and Jim Stack
DESIGNER: Brian Roeth
PRODUCTION COORDINATOR: Jennifer Wagner

F+W PUBLICATIONS, INC.

METRIC CONVERSION CHART

to convert	to	multiply by
Inches	Centimeters	2.54
Centimeters	Inches	0.4
Feet	Centimeters	30.5
Centimeters	Feet	0.03
Yards	Meters	0.9
Meters	Yards	1.1
Sq. Inches	Sq. Centimeters	6.45
Sq. Centimeters	Sq. Inches	0.16
Sq. Feet	Sq. Meters	0.09
Sq. Meters	Sq. Feet	10.8
Sq. Yards	Sq. Meters	0.8
Sq. Meters	Sq. Yards	1.2
Pounds	Kilograms	0.45
Kilograms	Pounds	2.2
Ounces	Grams	28.4
Grams	Ounces	0.035

INTRODUCTION

For most of us, time is a precious commodity. Between work, home and family duties, we have little or no time to unwind and take a deep breath. We, the editors of Popular Woodworking, have selected the projects in this book specifically for those moments when you discover a half a day, a whole day or (you lucky people!) an entire weekend that is available for woodworking.

As you peruse the table of contents, you will see the projects have been grouped according to the woodworking skills needed to build each project: beginner, intermediate and advanced. (Yes, even the advanced projects can be completed in a weekend.) You know what your own woodworking experiences have been and how comfortable you have felt. But, if you're unsure about your skill level, we've described some skills that we think categorize each skill level.

The *beginner* level of woodworking assumes a basic knowledge of woodworking terms and usage of hand tools, such as the ruler, saw, hammer, chisel, screwdriver and plane. Also, a working knowledge of power tools, such as the jig saw, drill press and hand drill is helpful. You possibly have the skills to build small boxes and bookshelves and know how to finish using a rub-on or brushed-on finish.

The *intermediate* level of woodworking assumes possession of beginner level skills, plus how to operate a table saw, band saw, stationary planer and jointer, lathe, biscuit joiner, pocket-hole drilling jig and doweling jig. You possibly have the skills to build bookshelves and cabinets and know how to finish using spray-on aerosol finishes.

The *advanced* level of woodworking includes all of the beginner and intermediate level skills, plus a knowledge of furniture design and how to make complex jointery. You possibly have the skills to make dressers, tables, kitchen cabinets and built-in bookcases and you are familiar with more types of finishing, such as stains, and can apply sprayed-on finishes using a spray gun.

Building a project from start to finish in a day or two is satisfying and rewarding and leaves you with a feeling of a job well done. Each project has materials lists, photos, technical drawings and clear text to help you make it correctly the first time. So pick out your project, find the time and enjoy woodworking!

PROJECT AUTHORS

RICHARD BLIZZARD, contributor: Versailles Tub With Obelisk Top. Copyright © Richard Blizzard 1999. Reproduced by kind permission of David & Charles Limited.

KARA GEBHART, managing editor, *Popular Woodworking* magazine: Simple CD Storage, Arts & Crafts Bookcase

CHRIS GLEASON, contributor: Music Cabinet

CHRISTOPHER SCHWARZ, executive editor, *Popular Woodworking* magazine: Two Frames, Santa's Cat

TROY SEXTON, contributor: Garage Golf Caddy, Simple Candle Boxes, Country Hanging Cupboard

STEVE SHANESY, editor and publisher, *Popular Woodworking* magazine: Angel-Face Ornament, Curly Maple Country Wall Shelf, Heirloom Photo Album, Greene & Greene Side Table

JIM STACK, acquisitions editor, Popular Woodworking Books: Handy Box, Curly Maple Desktop Organizer, Nightstand, Three-Legged Shop Stool, Boot Storage Bench

JIM STUARD, former associate editor, *Popular Woodworking* magazine: Chip-Carved Snowflake

MICHELLE TAUTE, former intern, *Popular Woodworking* magazine: Two-Faced Snowman

DAVID THIEL, senior editor, *Popular Woodworking* magazine: Old Plane Ornament, Bungalow Mailbox, Pocket Cigar Holder, Mantle Clock, Basic Bookcases, Shaker Firewood Box

CHRISTOPHER SCHWARZ and **KARA GEBHART**: 24-Hour Workbench

contents

■ BEGINNER LEVEL

BEGINNER

SIMPLE CD STORAGE | PAGE 6

POCKET CIGAR HOLDER | PAGE 36

■ INTERMEDIATE LEVEL

GARAGE GOLF CADDY | PAGE 38

■ ADVANCED LEVEL

MUSIC CABINET | PAGE 104

Simple CD Storage

BY KARA GEBHART

A CD's slim, compact design allows for all sorts of creativity when it comes to storing them. Tall CD towers and spinning CD cases have flooded the mega music stores.

Look under any passenger's car seat or flip down any driver's visor and you'll probably find some sort of CD storage device that involves plastic sleeves. And if you've ever built a desk for the home office, you've probably purchased plastic hardware designed to hold and organize your software and music collections.

Last year Senior Editor Christopher Schwarz was building an entertainment center and wasn't too excited about installing cheesy plastic rails designed to organize CDs into a handsomely built wooden project. Thinking there had to be a better way, he came up with one, opening all sorts of new doors for CD storage. All it takes is a table saw, a dado stack and some creativity.

The concept is simple: rows of dadoes specifically sized and spaced to hold the ends of CD cases. You can plow these dadoes into any piece of wood and then cut the result into all sorts of shapes — creating endless CD-storage possibilities. I liked Chris's idea, so I decided to stretch his concept. It worked great.

This concept lends itself to many different designs. At left is a wall-hung cherry design. The rack above has tapered maple sides and is the perfect size to go on the wall next to your computer.

Use dial calipers to determine the perfect width for your dadoes. Our dadoes ended up being 0.415" (a little less than $^7/_{16}$").

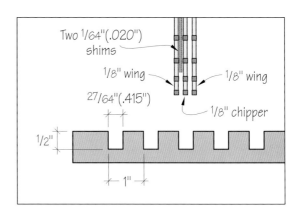

When cutting dadoes in smaller panels, screw a backer board to your miter gauge. This will decrease blowout.

Cutting the Perfect Dado

Before I even headed into the shop, I collected a bunch of CDs from around the office and measured their thicknesses with dial calipers. The thickness of the cases ranged from 0.393" (a little more than $^1/_4$") to 0.412" (a little less than $^7/_{16}$"). So I decided to make the first test dado 0.415" wide.

Next, I headed to the shop. To create a dado exactly 0.415" wide, I used two $^1/_8$" dado blades, a $^1/_8$" chipper and two 0.020" shims. Then, I cut a test dado $^1/_2$" deep in a $^3/_4$"-thick piece of scrap plywood. Next, I tested the 0.393"-thick case (the smallest one we found) and the 0.412"-thick case (the largest one we found) to see how they fit in the dado. To my surprise, the 0.415"-wide dado was a perfect match. The 0.412"-thick case slid in and out without any difficulty. And while the 0.393"-thick case drooped slightly in the dado, it stayed in place just fine.

Next, I tested how much wood I should leave between each dado. Too little wood created too fragile a project, while too much wood looked chunky. I

concluded that 1" (which includes the width of the dado) worked quite well, and allowed me to work with a simple whole number.

One more important fact: You need to cut dadoes and not grooves to make this work. Dadoes are cut across the grain; grooves are cut with the grain. When you cut dadoes, the CDs won't ever be pinched by the seasonal expansion and contraction of your board. Plus, the end result will be stronger. That's because wood is stronger along the grain than across it.

Rows and Rows of Dadoes

Before you start cutting your dadoes, you need to determine the shape of your CD rack. If it's simply going to be an insert inside a cabinet, measure what you need. But if it's going to be a rack hung on your wall, or a case you set on your desk, let your creative juices flow.

I drew up all kinds of sketches ranging from a simple rectangular shape with a contrasting wood frame to more complex shapes that involved angles

and curves. Just keep in mind the width of a CD case and the number of CD cases you want the project to hold (one across, two across, three across, etc.). CDs are just a touch less than 5" wide, and you want to allow about $^1/_4$" of space on either side so your fingers can get in there. So a CD rack for two columns of CDs should be $10^3/_4$" wide. For four columns, make it 21" wide and so on.

Once you have your shape (or shapes) in mind, prepare your stock and glue up any panels you might need. Make sure your panels are at least $^3/_4$" thick ($^7/_8$" is better), which will leave room for $^1/_2$"-deep dadoes.

Before you begin cutting dadoes in your good wood, make a few test cuts in a piece of scrap. Dadoes $^1/_2$" deep and 0.415" wide worked well for me, but your saw might have some more run-out or your shims might be slightly different from mine.

Once you've made your test cuts, decide how much wood you want to leave exposed on the top and bottom of your panels. For this curved wall-hung

CD rack, I decided to leave 2" on both the top and bottom.

Now screw a backing board to your slot miter gauge to stop the grain from blowing out at the end of each cut, as shown on the previous page. If your stock is narrow, then be sure to clamp a gauge block to your fence.

I set the fence at 2" and made the first cut. Be sure to go nice and slow. A little wobble here or there could create a too-big dado, causing your CD to fall out of its slot. After you've made your first cut, move your fence 1". This will leave a bit more than ½" of uncut wood between each dado. Make your second cut. Now, move your fence another 1". Make your third cut and so on. It's that easy.

Keep cutting dadoes until you run out of patience or run out of wood. Be sure to leave the same amount of exposed wood on the bottom as you did on the top, depending on your design.

Cutting Your Dadoes to Shape

Once all your dadoes are cut, sketch out the shape of your CD rack or, if it's going to be an insert, simply cut it to size. In the photo at right you can see a simple way to draw a curve.

Cut out your shapes using a band saw or jigsaw. If you're going to glue a frame to your rack, cut those pieces and glue them on the edges now. This is the time to be creative.

Now sand everything down. The curves can be a little tricky and might require a spokeshave or a spindle sander to get them looking good. Break all your edges with 150-grit sandpaper. Be forewarned: There are a lot of edges.

Before you apply a finish, you need to think about how you're going to hang your rack. I used a French cleat to hang my curved CD rack, adding a block at the bottom so the rack looks as if it's floating on the wall. You can

put two smaller CD racks back-to-back and attach them to a wooden stand to create a simple desktop CD case. Or you can simply attach a few cabinet hangers to the back of a wall-hung rack. How you hang it is up to you.

A clear finish gives your CD rack a contemporary look and allows the natu-

Cutting rows of dadoes in larger panels is an easy process. Simply cut one dado, move your fence 1" and then cut the next. Go slow.

Laying out curves often requires extra brad nails or extra hands. To lay out this curve, we marked the center of the panel and then measured 2½" down on either end. We then tapped three nails at each mark. One person held a thin piece of wood at each end nail, while the other person held the wood to the center nail and drew the curve.

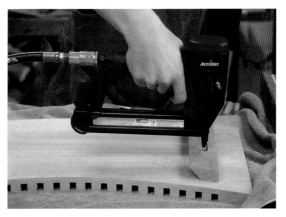

Here you can see I'm attaching the French cleat to the back of the curved wall-hung rack. This cleat, along with another block of wood that's attached further down the piece, will make the rack look like it's floating on the wall once hung.

ral color of what little wood is left to shine through.

While you wait for your finish to dry, start organizing your CD collection and pick your favorite ones to display. Make sure they're good ones, because with a project this cool they're guaranteed to get noticed.

Christmas Ornaments

OLD PLANE ORNAMENT

CHIP-CARVED SNOWFLAKE

SANTA'S CAT

TWO-FACED SNOWMAN

ANGEL-FACE ORNAMENT

OLD PLANE ORNAMENT

BY DAVID THIEL

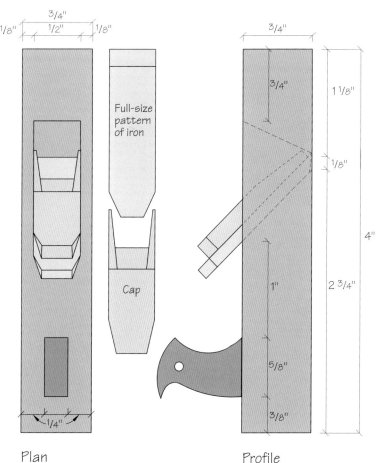

Plan

Profile

Nothing identifies a woodworker more than a wood plane, so why not mark your tree by hanging one (or a dozen) wooden planes on it?

The plane shown here is a jack plane made from four scraps. The body of the plane is mahogany, as is the cap and the handle. The "iron" is made of white oak, but if you have a piece of metal to use, it's even more authentic.

Cut the pieces to the sizes shown on the pattern, then cut the cap, iron and handle to shape using a scroll saw. The body of the plane is chiseled out as shown on the plan and profile views of the diagram to fit the cap and iron. Next, glue all the pieces in place. When you've got the plane assembled, spray on a couple of coats of clear finish, then add your hook and hang. It's an easy thing to personalize these planes with a special greeting and give them to friends and family as a special holiday gift from your own workshop.

TWO-FACED SNOWMAN

BY MICHELLE TAUTE

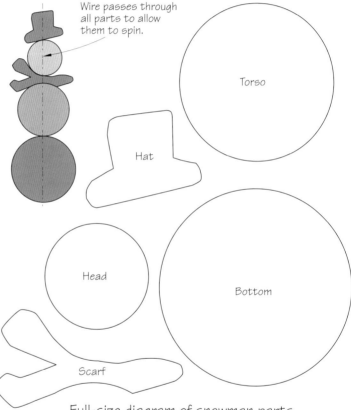

Wire passes through all parts to allow them to spin.

Torso

Hat

Head

Bottom

Scarf

Full-size diagram of snowman parts

This ornament puts a new spin on the traditional Christmas snowman. All the pieces are painted on both sides and can be spun to display a different hat, scarf or face.

The pieces are all cut from ¼" ply-wood scrap. Different thicknesses can be used, but keep in mind that the ornament needs to be fairly light to be easily supported by a tree branch. Trace the pieces onto the wood, using the drawing, or make your own modifications.

Cut out the pieces using a scroll saw. Then drill a small hole through the length of each piece. Take it slow. It's easy to drill out the side of one of the pieces. Next, paint all the pieces with the design of your choice. Just remember to vary each side so the pieces can be mixed and matched when spun.

Now it's time to assemble the piece. You need a piece of wire that is small enough to fit through the holes you drilled and 6" or 7" long. Put the snowman pieces on the wire one at a time. Then bend the wire over at the top and bottom to keep the pieces from coming off. You can use wire as a hanger or add a piece of ribbon.

SANTA'S CAT

BY CHRISTOPHER SCHWARZ

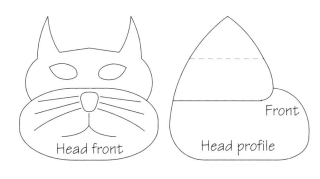

Head front

Head profile

Front

Tail

Full-size diagram
of head and tail

INCHES (MILLIMETERS)

REFERENCE	QUANTITY	PART	STOCK	THICKNESS	(mm)	WIDTH	(mm)	LENGTH	(mm)
A	1	body	walnut	1½	(38)	1½	(38)	3¾	(95)
B	2	legs	walnut	⅝	(16)	⅝	(16)	3	(76)
C	2	arms	walnut	⅝	(16)	⅝	(16)	2⅛	(54)
D	1	head	walnut	1½	(38)	1½	(38)	1½	(38)
E	1	tail	walnut	⅝	(16)	⅝	(16)	3	(76)
F	6	dowels	hardwood	¼	(6)	½	(13)		
G		inlay strips	maple	⅛	(3)	1	(25)	cut to length as needed	

13

Not every ornament on our family's tree has a Christmas theme. In fact, we have a lot of ornaments that have more to do with our pets than with the holidays. However, I'm sure that once my wife gets ahold of this cat it will have a red ribbon around its neck, a Santa Claus hat and a felt bag of presents.

Begin by cutting out a 1½" × 5" × 7" piece of walnut. Now, cut kerfs in the walnut block for the maple strips, or "stripes." Here's how: Set the height of your table saw's blade to ⅝". Now, make a cut through the width of the block. Turn the block over and make the same cut on the other side. Move your stop or fence ¼" and make the

same cuts on both sides. Repeat this procedure through about two-thirds the length of the block. Now glue ⅛" strips of maple into the kerfs. When the glue is dry, cut and shape the cat's parts on your band saw and disc sander. Carve the head from walnut

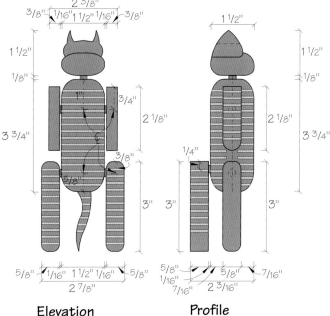

Elevation

Profile

scrap with a shop knife.

To assemble the cat, glue ¼" dowels into the arms, legs, tail and head. Then stick the dowels into ¼" holes in the body. Don't use glue here; this makes your cat poseable.

CHIP-CARVED SNOWFLAKE

BY JIM STUARD

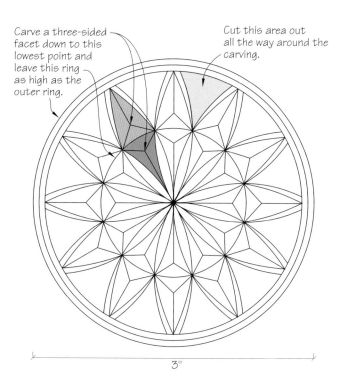

Carve a three-sided facet down to this lowest point and leave this ring as high as the outer ring.

Cut this area out all the way around the carving.

3"

Full-size diagram of snowflake ornament

Christmas in the Midwest involves removing lots of the stuff symbolized by this ornament from your driveway. It's more fun making snowflakes than shoveling them.

Start by cutting a $\frac{1}{4}$" × 3" × 3" piece of basswood. Paste the full-size pattern down onto the wood and cut out the circle. Drill clearance holes into the areas where you need to cut through the ornament. Use a scroll saw to cut the triangular-shaped holes first.

Chip carve the remaining areas of the ornament. The easiest way to start carving is to remove a little version of what the finished depression will look like. This will give you an idea of how the wood grain will react to the knife. The outer depressions are a little deeper than the inner ones. This gives you a sense of depth. Take your time and try to carve each depression evenly.

Finish the ornament by applying color and spraying a clear finish. Using gold paint, stipple (use the end of the brush pushed into the work) the edges of the ornament to highlight the carving. Pierce one of the cutouts and attach a wire for hanging.

ANGEL-FACE ORNAMENT

BY STEVE SHANESY

Full-scale pattern

If you are a traditionalist at the holidays, this Victorian-era ornament is perfect for you. First, browse through your photo album to find a photo that will fit the opening. Then head for the scroll saw.

For material, use ⅛" Baltic birch plywood. It provides strength where the cuts come close together. Before cutting, consider stacking three or four pieces so you cut multiple ornaments. If you stack them, glue the pieces together with a spray adhesive that will allow you to separate them easily when done. Then glue the design in place (or first make photocopies if you plan on more than one cutting).

Use a ¹⁄₁₆" drill bit to pierce the pattern to make inside cuts. Cut the outside first, then the inside. When done, separate and lightly sand, especially the edges.

To finish, first paint on a coat of dark red craft paint. When dry, lightly sand. Follow up with a light coat of gold paint. Apply this coat with a "dry" brush, a brush not fully loaded. Let some of the red show through.

Mount the photo using two pieces of round card stock, one in the shape of a doughnut to surround the photo, the other to cover the back. Glue both down.

Handy Box

BY JIM STACK

This toolbox is perfect for holding all those every-day tools that you use around the house — a tack hammer, screwdrivers, tape ruler, extra screws and nails, etc.

The techniques used to make this box are simple and fun. You can change the dimensions to suit your particular needs. For example, it would be a simple matter to make this box twice as big.

I prefer to see the wood that I use to build my projects, so I used a clear finish. Feel free to finish this project as you like — with paint, stain or whatever suits your needs.

Detail of folding the miter joint

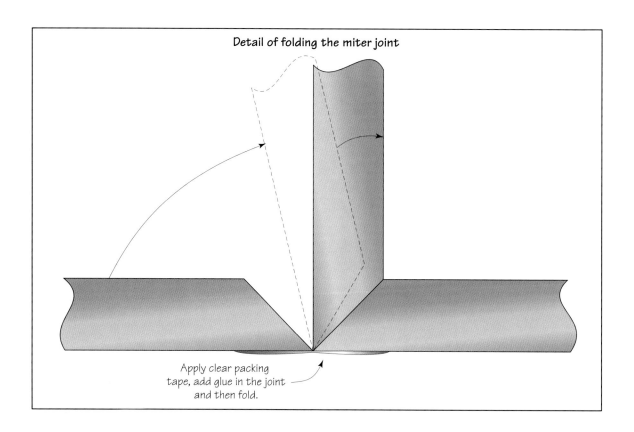

Apply clear packing
tape, add glue in the joint
and then fold.

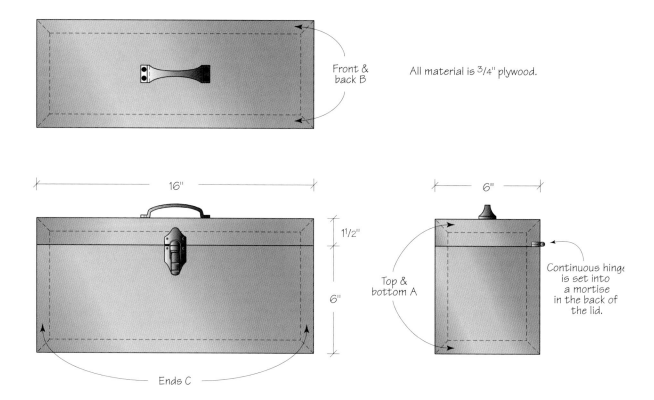

Front &
back B

All material is $3/4$" plywood.

16"

$1^{1}/2$"

6"

6"

Top &
bottom A

Ends C

Continuous hinge
is set into
a mortise
in the back of
the lid.

INCHES (MILLIMETERS)

REFERENCE	QUANTITY	PART	STOCK	THICKNESS	(mm)	WIDTH	(mm)	LENGTH	(mm)	COMMENTS
A	2	top & bottom	plywood	$3/4$	(19)	6	(152)	16	(406)	All edges have a 45° bevel.
B	2	front & back	plywood	$3/4$	(19)	$7^1/2$	(191)	16	(406)	All edges have a 45° bevel.
C	2	ends	plywood	$3/4$	(19)	6	(152)	$7^1/2$	(191)	All edges have a 45° bevel.

hardware & supplies

1 $3/16$" x $1^1/2$" x 16" (5mm x 38mm x 406mm)
  continuous hinge

1 drawbolt

1 screen door handle

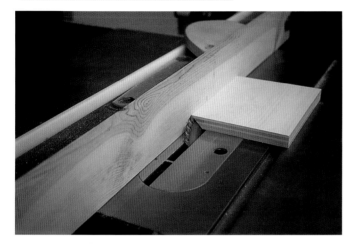

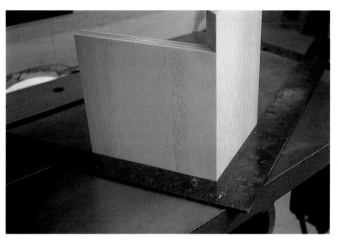

1 Cut all the parts to size as shown in the materials list. Then tilt the table saw blade to 45° and attach a sacrificial fence to the saw's fence. Adjust this setup until you can cut a 45° bevel on the edge of the box parts. This setup allows you to cut bevels on parts that have already been cut to size, which is easier than trying to cut all the parts to size and bevel them at the same time.

2 Double-check the 45° bevel to be sure that a perfect 90° corner is formed. This is critical for all the parts to join together squarely at glue-up time.

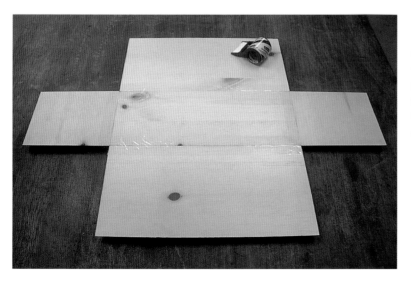

3 Lay out the bottom A, the front and back B and the two ends C faceup as shown. Use clear packing tape to tape the joints, creating a hinge. Be sure that the sharp edges of the bevels come together as cleanly as possible when you apply the tape.

BEVEL CUTS ON PLYWOOD EDGES

Be careful when cutting and handling plywood after you've cut bevels on the edges. Plywood edges are fragile and can be easily chipped or nicked. Also, I've received some nasty cuts from these edges as they are sharp!

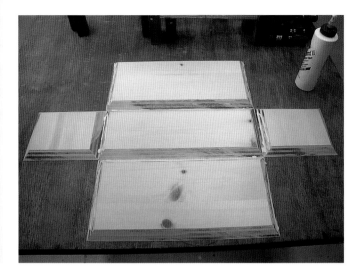

4 Turn the whole assembly face-down, then apply glue to all the edges that will be coming together when it's folded up.

5 You will need to use a few clamps to hold the side joints tightly. Don't use too much pressure, as that will distort the joint and cause it to open up at the sharp edges.

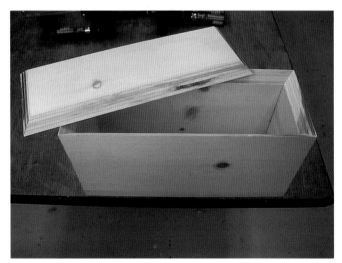

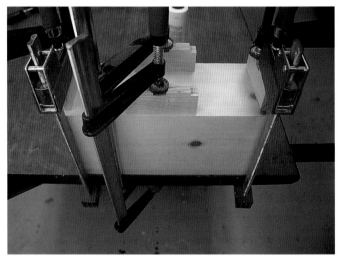

6 When the glue has dried, remove the clamps, apply glue to the remaining beveled edges and attach the top A.

7 Use blocks under the clamps to even out the pressure. At this point you might be wondering if you could tape the top to the assembly when all the parts are lying flat in step 3, and I say, "Yes, you could!" (I didn't because I simply got ahead of myself.) If I made this again, I would tape all the parts and fold up all six sides at one time.

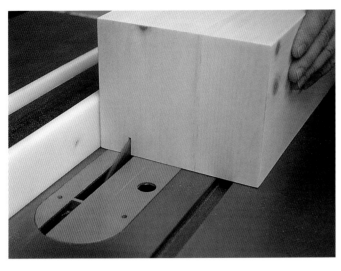

8 When the glue has dried, gently scrape or sand away any glue squeeze-out. Cut the lid off the box, using the table saw.

9 The lid will fit perfectly on the box using this technique.

10 Measure the thickness of the continuous hinge. Set the table saw fence to this measurement and make a through-cut.

11 Reset the fence to the width of the hinge leaf (this does not include the barrel of the hinge) and make the cleanup cut. This cut squares out the corner of the rabbet cut.

12 This is the finished cut. If your saw blade is a little dull (as mine is), you will have some burn marks on your wood. This is OK, as the hinge will cover these marks. (I guess I should get my saw blade sharpened!)

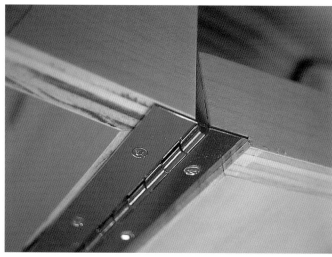

13 Install the hinge. If your cut is accurate, the hinge is lined up easily by holding the edge of the hinge leaf against the shoulder of the rabbet. By allowing the barrel of the hinge to extend beyond the edge of the box, the lid can be opened 180°.

14 This is a quick but neat and tidy way to install a hinge. You can now install the drawbolt and screen door handle.

15 When you've finished the box, the corners will have a nice, clean look. The miter joint is a strong joint. The gluing surface is large, and no splines or biscuits are needed.

Bungalow Mailbox

BY DAVID THIEL

This project was by request. As I live in the 'burbs and have to walk to the curb to pick up my bills, a mailbox mounted next to my front door would be purely decorative. But a friend lucky enough to have postal delivery right to his door asked if I could come up with an appropriate design for his Arts & Crafts–style bungalow home.

After a little research I settled on a design reminiscent of the work of Charles Rennie Mackintosh. Arguably Scotland's greatest 20th-century architect and designer, Mackintosh inspired much of the European Arts & Crafts movement during the early 1900s. A stylized flower motif is found on many of his pieces.

INCHES (MILLIMETERS)

REFERENCE	QUANTITY	PART	STOCK	THICKNESS	(mm)	WIDTH	(mm)	LENGTH	(mm)
A	2	sides	white oak	3/8	(10)	4 1/2	(114)	11	(279)
B	1	front	white oak	3/8	(10)	6	(152)	9	(229)
C	1	back	white oak	3/8	(10)	5 1/4	(133)	13	(330)
D	1	bottom	white oak	3/8	(10)	3 11/16	(94)	5 7/8	(149)
E	1	lid	white oak	3/8	(10)	5	(127)	7 3/4	(197)
F	1	applied detail	white oak	1/8	(3)	6	(152)	9	(229)
G	2	magazine hooks	copper pipe	3/4	(19)			14	(356)

hardware & supplies

1 continuous hinge

The bottom fits into the front and back pieces using a tongue-and-groove method. The sides are not attached to the bottom, and in fact, the bottom is cut to allow a 1/16" gap on either side. Should water happen to get into the mailbox, these gaps will allow it to escape rather than pool up in the bottom.

Mostly Glue

The joinery for the box is primarily glue and butt joints, utilizing the long-grain-to-long-grain orientation of the sides, back and front. The bottom, however, sits in a tongue-and-groove joint between the front and back pieces to allow the wood to move.

After cutting the pieces according to the materials list, cut a 1/4" × 1/8" rabbet on the underside of the two long edges of the bottom D. Then, cut the dadoes

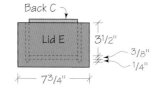

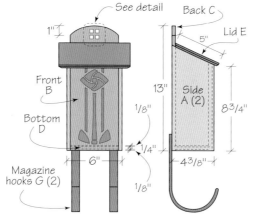

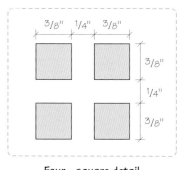

Four - square detail

on the inside bottom of the front B and back C by setting the rip fence for 1/2" and the blade height to 3/16".

Adding the Angles

Now, cut the sides A of the mailbox on an angle so you can attach the mailbox to your house without cramming a tool inside the box. The sides A slope at a 25° angle with the front edge measuring 9" tall and the back edge 11" tall.

Now, cut the chamfer on the underside of the lid E. The front B and two sides A are chamfered at a 45° angle on the table saw, leaving a 3/16" flat edge to the top of the lid E. The back edge of the lid is cut at a 25° angle to mate with the box's back.

Detailing the Back

To add another Mackintosh feature, I cut a four-square pattern centered in

the top of the curved back C.

First, mark the location of the four-square pattern as shown on the diagram. Use a 3/8" drill bit to remove most of the waste from the squares. Then use a chisel and a triangular file to clean up the cuts. To make the curve, draw a 6" radius along the top edge of the back C and cut to the mark on the band saw.

After sanding, you're ready to glue up the box. The front B is set back 1/4" on the sides A, while the back C is flush to the back edge. The bottom D is left loose in the assembly.

Now, using the full-size pattern, cut out the applied detail F from 1/8" stock on the scroll saw.

Finishing Touches

Before gluing the flower to the box, stain the box a rustic-looking gray-brown by

The top is chamfered on three edges and angle-cut on the back edge. By moving my rip fence to the left of the blade, my right-tilt saw is able to make the cuts safely, allowing the waste to fall away from the blade.

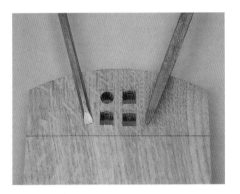

After drilling the holes, use a $^1/_8$" chisel and a triangular file to clean up the hole. The top left hole is shown after drilling, while the two lower holes have been completed.

applying a black aniline dye wash. The wash was made by diluting the dye eight-to-one with denatured alcohol. I then colored the flower and stem pieces with undiluted aniline dye. Attach the flower pieces using cyanoacrylate glue. To finish, use a coat of spar urethane for outdoor protection.

The final tasks are installing a small jewelry box continuous hinge for the lid and installing the copper magazine hooks G. I made the hooks from a couple of pieces of $^3/_4$" copper tubing. Flatten the piece with a dead-blow hammer, then use a ball-peen hammer to add a dimpled, hand-hammered appearance. I then "antiqued" the copper using a product called Modern Options Patina Green. The product quickly adds a nice green patina.

Now screw the two hooks to the back, and the mailbox is ready to hang.

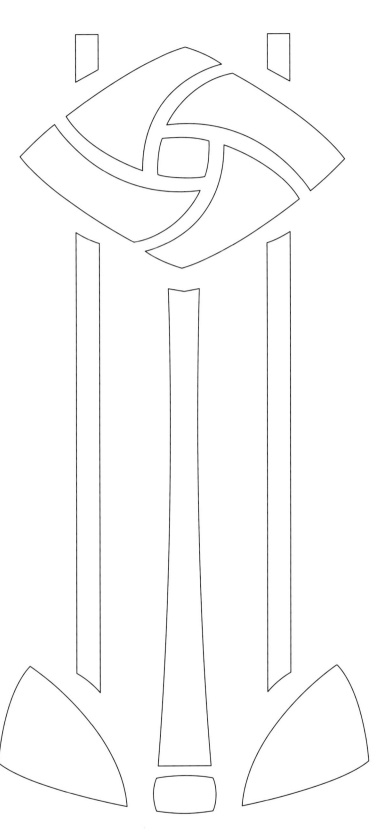

Curly Maple Desktop Organizer

BY JIM STACK

If you're like me, keeping things organized is a challenge. This project will help you create a place to store a few things, therefore keeping your desktop a little neater. This organizer is made of curly maple, which makes the piece visually attractive. The basics of biscuit joinery are all that are needed to build this project. The shelf unit is assembled with biscuits, as is the drawer. Before final assembly, all the parts are sanded and finished.

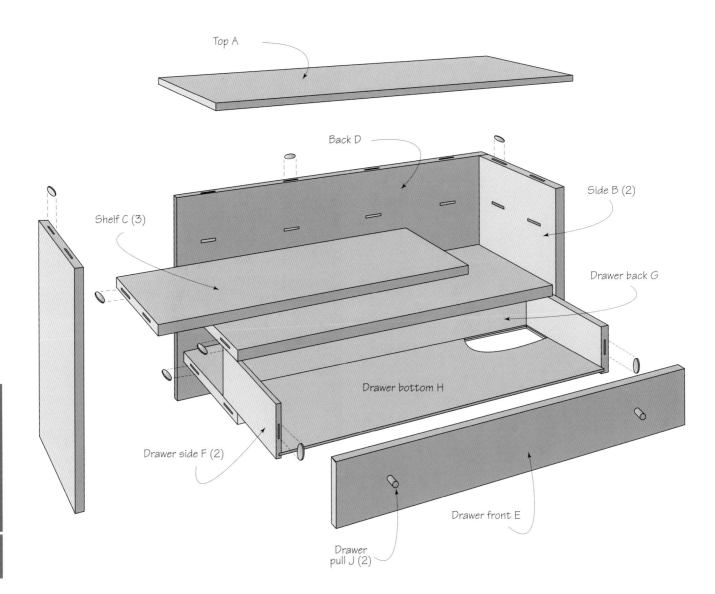

Top A

Back D

Side B (2)

Shelf C (3)

Drawer back G

Drawer bottom H

Drawer side F (2)

Drawer front E

Drawer
pull J (2)

INCHES (MILLIMETERS)

REFERENCE	QUANTITY	PART	STOCK	THICKNESS	(mm)	WIDTH	(mm)	LENGTH	(mm)
A	1	top	curly maple	³/₄	(19)	10	(254)	30	(762)
B	2	sides	curly maple	³/₄	(19)	9³/₄	(248)	17¹/₄	(438)
C	3	shelves	curly maple	³/₄	(19)	8³/₄	(222)	26¹/₂	(673)
D	1	back	birch ply	³/₄	(19)	14¹/₄	(362)	27¹/₂	(699)
E	1	drawer front	curly maple	³/₄	(19)	3	(76)	26¹/₂	(673)
F	2	drawer sides	maple	¹/₂	(13)	3	(76)	7³/₄	(197)
G	1	drawer back	maple	¹/₂	(13)	2¹/₄	(57)	25¹/₂	(648)
H	1	drawer bottom	luan ply	¹/₄	(6)	8	(203)	26	(660)
J	2	drawer pulls	oak dowel	³/₄ dia.	(19)				

hardware & supplies

36   No. 20 biscuits

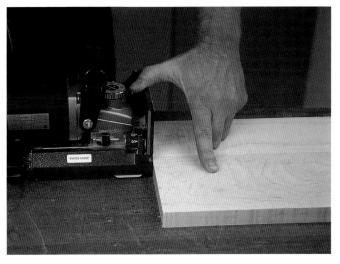

1 Lay the two sides B side by side and cut all the biscuit slots at the same time. This will ensure that the shelves C will be level and the project will be square when assembled.

2 Lay the shelves C faceup on a flat surface when cutting the slots. The bottoms of the shelves will then be located correctly with the slots that have been cut in the sides.

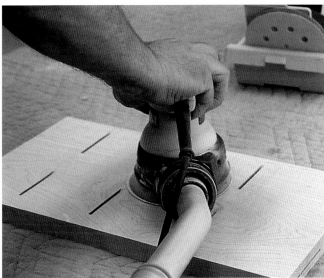

4 After the slots have been cut and you've determined that the parts fit together properly, finish-sand all the parts.

3 Stand the top A on its back edge and cut the slots that line up with the back D. Next, cut the slots in the top A where the sides B will attach to the top, using the layout square. To locate the slots, dry assemble the base of the project and measure the distance between the slots in the tops of the sides B. Transfer this measurement to the top A, making sure the top will be centered on the base.

5 To keep the finish out of the slots, cover them with masking tape. Finish the parts.

6 Let the finish cure overnight, then assemble the project. (You will find it easier to clean up any glue that oozes out of the joints, because the unit was finished prior to assembly.)

7 The back D is screwed to the base. Note that the screw is inserted at a slight angle so it won't cause a bulge on the inside of the project.

8 Glue the top A in place.

9 Lay out all the drawer parts in order, and label them using an orienting triangle. Remember that the drawer sides F will capture the front E and back G when the drawer is assembled.

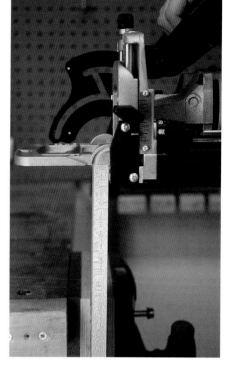

10 Mark the location of the biscuits and cut the slots in the front E and back parts G. When making drawers, use the largest biscuits you can. For this drawer, use No.20 biscuits.

11 Cut the slots into the sides F.

13 This photo shows a detail of the finished drawer and white oak $^3/_4$" drawer pull J. Any wooden dowel would make a nice, simple pull for the drawer.

12 Assemble the drawer. You can either use a captured bottom H (as shown here) or cut the bottom of the back G off. Finish the drawer and the bottom H. Slide the bottom H into the assembled drawer.

Two Frames

BY CHRISTOPHER SCHWARZ

If you're new to woodworking or to Arts & Crafts furniture, you should try your hand at building a frame for a picture or mirror first. You'll learn how to cut a mortise-and-tenon joint without the fear of blowing an entire morris chair. You'll learn how to peg this joint to make it even more durable. And you'll get a feel for working with white oak and get to experiment with finishes.

The picture frame featured here was built to hold a photo in a mat that measures 16" × 20", which is a standard size. It's a simple matter to adjust the measurements of the stiles and rails if your photo or painting is bigger. I built this frame after a visit to the Gamble House in Pasadena, California, which was designed by the Greene brothers. On the tour of the house it became evident that one of the keys to their designs was that everything be in threes: three rails, three cutouts, three inlays. So with that in mind, I designed this traditional Arts & Crafts frame.

The second piece is a mirror frame designed to hold a standard 24" × 24" mirror, which is available at most home center stores. This design was taken from an actual mirror that was featured at an auction held by Treadway Gallery of Cincinnati, Ohio. Construction of both frames is similar, but because they use different thicknesses of wood, I'll cover each one separately.

Picture Frame

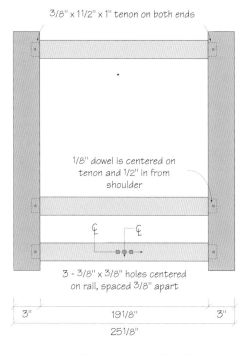

3/8" x 11/2" x 1" tenon on both ends

1/8" dowel is centered on tenon and 1/2" in from shoulder

3 - 3/8" x 3/8" holes centered on rail, spaced 3/8" apart

¢   ¢

3"   191/8"   3"
251/8"

3/4"

1/4"   1/2"

1/4"

Mirror Frame Corbel Detail

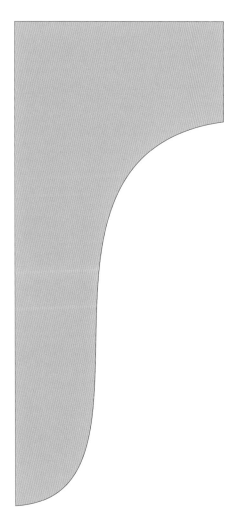

Mirror Frame

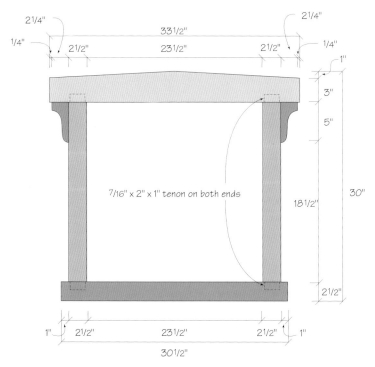

21/4"   331/2"   21/4"

1/4"   21/2"   231/2"   21/2"   1/4"

1"

3"

5"

7/16" x 2" x 1" tenon on both ends

181/2"   30"

21/2"

1"   21/2"   231/2"   21/2"   1"
301/2"

Picture Frame

The first step is to choose your wood. With picture frames you have to remember that you've got only a few sticks of wood so you want to show the best grain possible. However, that being said, you also don't want the grain to be so wild that it competes with or outshines the artwork it's supposed to display. So look for ray flake that is somewhere in the middle.

Cut all your pieces to size and get ready to cut your mortise-and-tenon joints. The rule of thumb is to cut your tenons to be half as thick as your wood. So if your wood is $3/4$" thick, your tenons should be $3/8$" thick. For wood this narrow, you should cut $1/4$" shoulders on the edges. I usually make all my tenons 1" long. So the tenons on the rails B should measure $3/8$" thick, $1\frac{1}{2}$" wide and 1" long. I like to cut my tenons using a dado stack in a table saw.

Now, cut your mortises. You want your mortises to be a little deeper than your tenons so the tenon won't bottom out in your mortise. So your mortises should measure $3/8$" thick, $1\frac{1}{2}$" wide and $1\frac{1}{16}$" long. I like to use a hollow chisel mortiser, but it's not necessary. If you own a drill press, you can cut these mortises using a $3/8$" Forstner bit and a fence clamped to your drill press's table. Then square the corners using a chisel.

While you're set up for mortising, make the three square cutouts on the bottom rail.

Now, cut the $1/4$"-deep by $1/2$"-wide rabbet on the backs of the stiles A and rails B to hold the picture in place. You'll have to stop the rabbet in the stiles, but this is a simple thing to do with a rabbeting bit in a router table.

Now, test the fit of everything and clamp your frame without glue to make sure everything fits and closes tightly. When you're satisfied, put glue in the mortises and clamp your picture frame. Make sure your frame is square by measuring the frame's diagonals (from corner to corner). If the diagonal measurements are not identical, place a clamp across the two corners that were longer. Apply a slight bit of pressure and check your diagonals again.

When the glue is dry, remove the frame from the clamps. Now, peg your tenons for additional strength. I like to use $1/4$" oak dowels C. The size of store-bought dowels is rarely consistent, so first cut some holes in scrap pieces of wood to test how your dowels fit. I like to use a drill press for this operation. When you've found the perfect bit, drill the holes about $5/8$" deep into your frame. The holes don't need to go all the way through. Put a little glue into the hole and hammer the dowel home. Cut any excess flush to the stiles.

Now finish-sand the frame. Start with 100 grit, then move up to 120 and finish with 150. This frame is finished with a simple mahogany gel stain. After your stain dries, cover it with three coats of a clear finish. Install the glass, photo and mat, and hold them in the rabbet using mirror clips, which screw to the back side of your frame.

Mirror Frame

This frame is a little more work, but the operations are all the same. After you cut your pieces to size, cut your tenons on the ends of the stiles F. Because this stock is $7/8$" thick, you'll need to make your tenons $7/16$" thick. So your tenons should measure $7/16$" thick, 2" wide and 1" long. Your mortises should be $7/16$" thick, 2" wide and $1\frac{1}{16}$" long. Once you've got your joints cut, turn your attention to the top rail D.

The top rail D slopes from 4" high in the middle to 3" on the ends. Mark this on the rail and make the cut on a band saw. Clean up the cut on your jointer.

Now, cut the rabbet on the back of the pieces to hold the mirror in place. I cut a $1/8$"-deep by $1/4$"-wide rabbet using a rabbeting bit in a router table.

Test the fit of all your joints and then glue up your frame. When the glue is dry, peg the joints. Cut out the two corbels G according to the pattern in the diagram and finish-sand all your parts. Glue the corbels G in place (flush to the back side of the frame) and finish the frame.

I combined two dyes to get this dark color — a brown dye and a deep red dye. Then I followed it with three coats of a clear finish.

When the finish is dry, put the mirror in its rabbet and use mirror clips to hold it in place.

INCHES (MILLIMETERS)

REFERENCE	QUANTITY	PART	STOCK	THICKNESS	(mm)	WIDTH	(mm)	LENGTH	(mm)	COMMENTS
PICTURE FRAME										
A	2	stiles		$3/4$	(19)	3	(76)	$26\frac{1}{8}$	(664)	
B	3	rails		$3/4$	(19)	2	(51)	$21\frac{1}{8}$	(537)	1" tenon both ends
C	6	dowels		$1/8$ dia.	(3)			$3/4$	(19)	
MIRROR FRAME										
D	1	top rail		$7/8$	(22)	4	(102)	$33\frac{1}{2}$	(851)	
E	1	bottom rail		$7/8$	(22)	$2\frac{1}{2}$	(64)	$30\frac{1}{2}$	(775)	
F	2	stiles		$7/8$	(22)	$2\frac{1}{2}$	(64)	$25\frac{1}{2}$	(648)	1" tenon both ends
G	2	corbels		$3/4$	(19)	$2\frac{1}{4}$	(57)	5	(127)	
H	4	dowels		$1/8$ dia.	(3)			$3/4$	(19)	

Pocket Cigar Holder

BY DAVID THIEL

Cigar aficionados enjoy a good cigar a lot more when it's not bent or broken. This sturdy cigar keeper protects two $6\frac{1}{4}" \times 50$ ring ($\frac{1}{64}" =$ 1 ring size) cigars and shows the world a bit of style.

The box construction is simple. A block is cut in half, the center is hollowed, and then the halves are glued back together. But start by choosing your wood for the most attractive grain pattern.

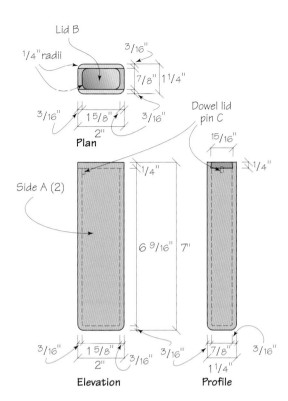

Plan

Lid B

1/4" radii

3/16"

7/8" 1 1/4"

3/16" 1 5/8" 3/16"

2"

Dowel lid pin C

15/16"

1/4"

1/4"

Side A (2)

6 9/16" 7"

3/16" 1 5/8" 3/16" 3/16" 7/8" 3/16"

2" 1 1/4"

Elevation   **Profile**

INCHES (MILLIMETERS)

REFERENCE	QUANTITY	PART	STOCK	THICKNESS	(mm)	WIDTH	(mm)	LENGTH	(mm)
A	2	sides	maple	5/8	(16)	2 1/16	(52)	7 1/16	(179)
B	1	lid	maple	1/4	(6)	1 1/16	(27)	2 1/16	(52)
C	1	dowel lid pin	hardwood	1/8 dia.	(3)			1/2	(13)

1 Saw the stock in half to the sizes given. Then, make the slot for the lid B by cutting a 3/16" by 3/8" deep rabbet on the inside top edge of each side A.

2 The lid B moves in a sliding dovetail, so set up your router table with a 9° dovetail bit to cut one side of a 1/4"-high dovetail on the lip formed earlier by the rabbet cut.

3 Now, cut out the inside space for the cigars. First, make a template using 1/4" plywood with a 3/4" × 1 1/2" solid strip screwed to the underside. A hole cut in the 1/4" plywood will guide your router using a template guide attached to your router base. Taking your template guide into account, make the template hole to remove material from each side A to form a 7/16" × 1 3/4" × 7" pocket. Note that one end of the pocket will be open-ended, the result of the earlier rabbet cut.

4 Clamp the side A to the template. Use multiple passes of increasing depths with a 1/2" fluting bit to form the interior curved edge of each box half.

5 To remove the remaining material, use a second template guide that is 1/2" larger in diameter than the first, or make a second template that's similar to the first (but with a 1/2" smaller opening), and a straight bit.

6 Glue the sides A together.

7 Sand the sides and bottom flush and square. Then use a 1/4" roundover bit to shape all the edges of the box, except the top.

8 Cut the lid material in a long strip. Then run the edges with the dovetail bit to form the lid B. Test the fit and sand as necessary. Then cut the lid B to length and finish sanding the entire box with the lid in place.

9 Finish the box to seal and protect the wood. Use a finish that won't impart any odor to the stored cigars.

10 Install the small dowel lid pin C to prevent the lid B from falling out. Drill a 1/8"-deep hole on the underside of the lid. The hole is set in as far as the side of the keeper is thick and is centered front to back.

11 With the lid B on the box, but open most of the way, glue the dowel C into the hole using angled tweezers or needle-nosed pliers. Your keeper is complete.

If you'd like to make one with an accent stripe as shown in the photo, simply adjust the thickness of the sides and the depth of the cuts for the interior.

Garage Golf Caddy

BY TROY SEXTON

Although my shop keeps me busy, I still find time for hunting in the woods surrounding our home, fly fishing and, lately, swinging some iron with one of my favorite golfing partners: my son, Josh.

Much like woodworking, as Josh and I have become more active in the sport of golf, our collection of golf-related paraphernalia has grown. Clubs, balls, tees and spikes began cluttering our family's garage and back hallway. (And you thought woodworking was expensive?) I decided a quick but sturdy cabinet would be the perfect garage storage solution.

This cabinet holds two golf bags with all our stuff at the ready for those days when the weather is perfect and cabinetmaking can wait. We just pull our truck forward a bit, load it up and head for the course.

This project is easy enough to build on a Saturday, ensuring ample time for the links on Sunday. Basically, the project works like this: The sides are dadoed to accept the top and bottom. The two adjustable shelves hang on pins between the two partitions. Everything else is assembled using nails and glue.

At first, I was a little concerned with how stable the cabinet would be without a back. But as long as your dadoes are tight, I can assure you that your cabinet will be rock solid. The top back splash does an excellent job of adding rigidity to this open cabinet.

Selecting the perfect wood for a project is a lot like selecting the perfect iron to put a ball on the green. I chose oak for its durability, strength and relatively inexpensive cost.

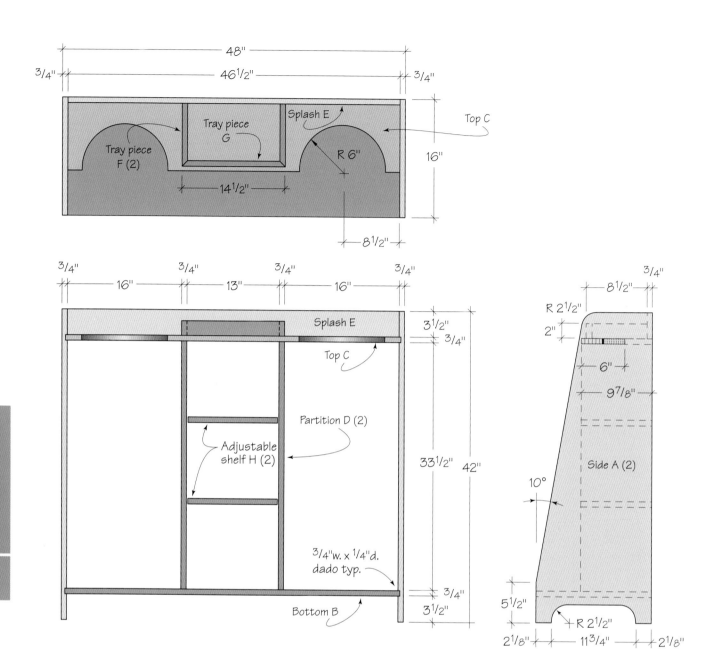

INCHES (MILLIMETERS)

REFERENCE	QUANTITY	PART	STOCK	THICKNESS	(mm)	WIDTH	(mm)	LENGTH	(mm)	COMMENTS
A	2	sides	oak	3/4	(19)	16	(406)	42	(1067)	
B	1	bottom	oak	3/4	(19)	16	(406)	47	(1194)	
C	1	top	oak	3/4	(19)	10	(254)	47	(1194)	rip front at 10°
D	2	partitions	oak	3/4	(19)	9⁷/₈	(251)	33¹/₂	(851)	
E	1	splash	oak	3/4	(19)	3¹/₂	(89)	46¹/₂	(1181)	
F	2	tray pieces	oak	3/4	(19)	2	(51)	8¹/₂	(216)	mitered
G	1	tray piece	oak	3/4	(19)	2	(51)	14¹/₂	(368)	mitered
H	2	adjustable shelves	oak	3/4	(19)	9³/₄	(248)	12³/₄	(324)	

hardware & supplies

5mm shelf pins

finish nails

Here I'm dry fitting the case of my garage golf caddy. Tight fitting dadoes will ensure a stable project. And before someone writes me a letter, let me just say that I know that sandals are not a good choice for woodworking footwear.

The 6"-radius half circles on the top piece are simple to cut out with a jigsaw. Your golf bag will neatly nest in this opening.

Hitting the Fairway

First, cut all your parts to size according to the materials list. Make the miter cuts on the three tray pieces F and G that make up the ball tray on the top.

Next, lay out your two 6"-radius half circles on the top C, as shown in the diagram. These half circles cradle your golf bags. Your best bet is to use a piece of string attached to a pencil to lay out these curves. With the line marked on the top, cut the curve using your jigsaw.

Now, cut the $\frac{3}{4}$" × $\frac{1}{4}$" dadoes in the sides A to receive the top C and bottom B. Lay your dadoes out according to the diagram. You can either use a dado set in your table saw or a straight bit chucked into your router to make these cuts. Dry fit the top C and bottom B into your sides A, making sure the fit is tight. As I said earlier, a tight fit will ensure a stable cabinet. No need to take a bogie here.

Once your dadoes are cut, lay out the angles on your two sides A according to the diagram. I cut these angles using my jigsaw, but a band saw will work, too.

Now it's time to drill the holes for the shelf pins, so grab your drill and a 5mm drill bit. I use 5mm shelf supports instead of $\frac{1}{4}$" shelf supports because the 5mm supports require smaller holes that don't stand out as much. You can purchase these supports at most woodworking stores or from catalogs. Woodcraft Supply, Lee Valley Tools and

Woodworker's Supply are all good sources for this item. Don't forget that you'll also need a metric drill bit, which is also easy to find in most catalogs these days.

The holes are spaced 2" apart. Drill 12 sets of 5mm holes on the inside face of each partition D for maximum shelving flexibility.

Nearing the Bar

Before I assemble anything, I like to sand my projects to 180 grit. Sanding now will be much easier than waiting to sand after the project is put together.

First, assemble the top C and bottom B to one of the sides A. Then add the other side A. Next, using a finish nailer and glue, add the two partitions D. Now add the splash E. You could use pocket-hole screws to attach the splash to the back side, but I stuck with my nailer and glue and it's held up to abuse just fine.

Next comes the mitered tray pieces F and G. Again, I just used my brad nailer and glue to assemble these. Attach the tray to the top C, using glue and a couple of brads from underneath the top. Finally, place your adjustable shelves

H in between the two partitions D.

Once everything is assembled and dry, sand all your front edges and then spray the entire piece with a couple of clear coats of lacquer or whatever finish you are most comfortable with.

Now it's time to hit the pro shop and fill all the shelf space you've just created.

Place your partitions using the diagram, then nail them in with a finish nailer. A little glue helps, too.

Nightstand

BY JIM STACK

After you've comfortably settled into your bed for the evening, you can read that great classic novel by the light of a lamp sitting on this nightstand. (There's also room for some cookies and hot chocolate.) The drawer has room for a pencil and a notebook or a journal.

INTERMEDIATE

43

hardware & supplies

14 No. 20 biscuits
14 1¼" drywall screws

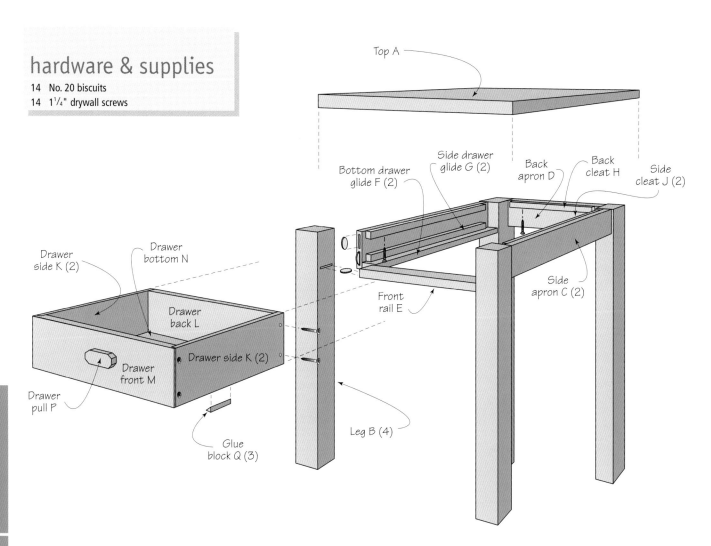

Top A

Bottom drawer glide F (2)

Side drawer glide G (2)

Back apron D

Back cleat H

Side cleat J (2)

Drawer side K (2)

Drawer bottom N

Drawer back L

Drawer side K (2)

Front rail E

Side apron C (2)

Drawer front M

Drawer pull P

Glue block Q (3)

Leg B (4)

INCHES (MILLIMETERS)

REFERENCE	QUANTITY	PART	STOCK	THICKNESS	(mm)	WIDTH	(mm)	LENGTH	(mm)	COMMENTS
A	1	top	sugar pine	1	(25)	18	(457)	22	(559)	
B	4	legs	sugar pine	2½	(64)	2½	(64)	27¼	(692)	
C	2	side aprons	sugar pine	1	(25)	5	(127)	12	(305)	
D	1	back apron	sugar pine	1	(25)	5	(127)	15	(381)	
E	1	front rail	sugar pine	1	(25)	2½	(64)	15	(381)	
F	2	bottom drawer glides	soft maple	¾	(19)	2	(51)	11½	(292)	
G	2	side drawer glides	soft maple	¾	(19)	¾	(19)	11½	(292)	
H	1	back cleat	soft maple	1	(25)	1	(25)	14½	(368)	
J	2	side cleats	soft maple	1	(25)	1	(25)	11½	(292)	
K	2	drawer sides	soft maple	½	(13)	4	(102)	14	(356)	
L	1	drawer back	soft maple	½	(13)	3¼	(83)	14	(356)	
M	1	drawer front	sugar pine	1	(25)	4	(102)	15	(381)	rough-sawn pine
N	1	drawer bottom	birch ply	¼	(6)	14½	(368)	13¾	(349)	
P	1	drawer pull	sugar pine	¾	(19)	1½	(38)	3¼	(83)	
Q	3	glue blocks	soft maple	½	(13)	½	(13)	3	(76)	

1 Biscuits work well for aligning and holding this project together. Make the slots for the aprons C and D and the front rail E. Be sure all the legs B have slots on two adjacent sides.

2 Glue up two legs B (a front leg and a back leg) and a side apron D to create a side assembly. Make two of these assemblies.

3 Glue the two side assemblies together using the back apron D and the front rail E. Then, glue on the cleats H and J for attaching the top A.

4 Preassemble the runner assemblies using a bottom drawer glide F and a side drawer glide G. Make two of these assemblies. Then, glue these runner assembies in place. Be sure the side runners are slightly proud of the inside of the front legs. This will allow the drawer to slide in and out without rubbing the legs. The bottom drawer guides should be level with the front rail. Make sure the runner assemblies are parallel with each other.

5 Attach the top A with 1¼" drywall screws through the mounting cleats H and J. Do not use glue. Then fit the drawer to the opening. It is easier to fit each drawer side individually, making the necessary adjustments as needed before assembling the drawer.

6 The drawer front M has rabbets on each end that accept the sides K. Set the table saw fence at ½" (including the blade thickness) and the blade height at ½" (the thickness of the drawer sides). Stand the drawer front M on end with the inside face against the fence and make the first cut for the rabbet in each end.

7 Lay the drawer front M faceup and make the second rabbet cut as shown here. (Always use a scrap of wood to test your cuts.)

8 Assemble the drawer using 1¼" drywall screws. Attach the sides to the drawer front M and the drawer back L. Slide the drawer bottom N into place and secure it in place using three 1¼" drywall screws inserted through the bottom into the bottom of the back L. Then, using glue, attach the three glue blocks Q to the bottom of the drawer. Locate two at each side of the drawer and one at the front of the drawer. These blocks help strenthen the drawer. Make any fitting adjustments needed using a belt sander and/or a block plane.

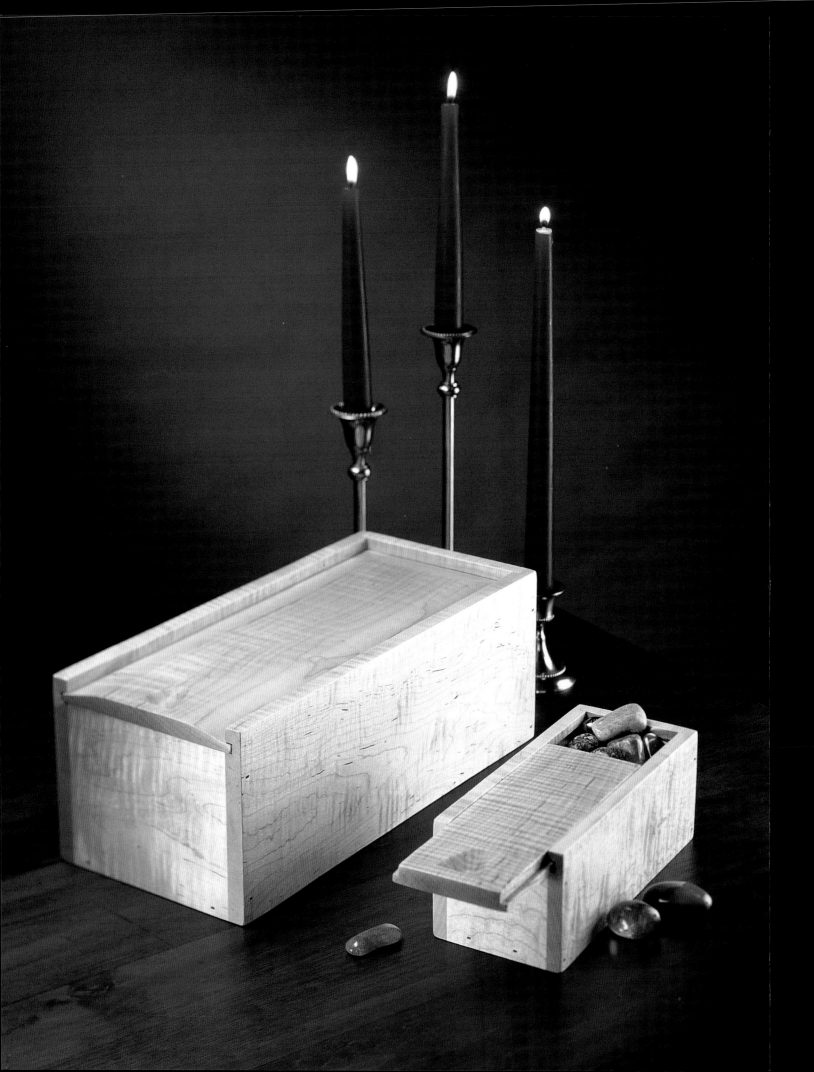

Simple Candle Boxes

BY TROY SEXTON

Every time my wife and I go antique shopping, Terri invariably buys a candle box. She loves them, which is why we have them all over the house. Look in any of our cabinets or on any of our table-tops and you'll likely find one of these simple boxes being used for storage or decoration.

As our collection of candle boxes from an-tique shows grew, it dawned on me: I should be building them. And so I did. You can build several of these classic boxes in a day, and they're a great idea for last-minute, homemade gifts. They look really nice on a shelf, and they're a great way to hide all the things you don't want lying about, such as spare change. And here's the best part: They're simple to build.

LARGE BOX

INCHES (MILLIMETERS)

REFERENCE	QUANTITY	PART	STOCK	THICKNESS	(mm)	WIDTH	(mm)	LENGTH	(mm)
A	1	front	maple	1/2	(13)	4³/₈	(111)	5	(127)
B	1	back	maple	1/2	(13)	5	(127)	5¹/₂	(140)
C	2	sides	maple	1/2	(13)	5	(127)	13¹/₂	(343)
D	1	bottom	maple	1/2	(13)	5	(127)	12¹/₂	(318)
E	1	lid	maple	1/2	(13)	5¹/₂	(140)	13¹/₄	(337)

BUILDING THE SMALL BOX

Following are some sizes and dimensions that will be helpful when building the small candle box.

• Overall dimensions:
  3" high by 8" wide by 3³/₈" deep

• Built using ³/₈" stock

• Rabbets on side pieces: ¹/₄" x ³/₈"

• Grooves on side pieces and back:
  ³/₁₆" deep by ¹/₄"

• Rabbets on lid: ¹/₈" x ¹/₄"

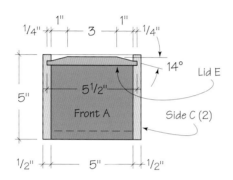

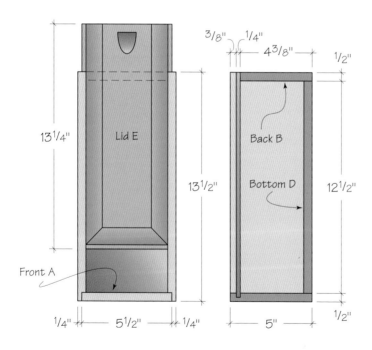

Some Thoughts on Size

Before you begin, you need to choose the size of your candle box. The illustration, materials list and the instructions that follow offer the details you need to build the large box that's shown in the picture. This large box has a one-piece bottom. But if you choose to build an even larger box, then you should consider a two-board bottom that's simply shiplapped together. The shiplap joint takes care of any shrinking or swelling that might occur with seasonal humidity changes.

The sliding lid on your candle box also will differ depending on the size candle box you choose to build. My large candle box has a beveled top, while my smaller candle box has a rabbeted top. I cut my bevels using my table saw, so when building smaller candle boxes that require a smaller top, a rabbet cut is the safer cut to make.

Once you've determined the size of your candle box, the construction part is easy. The back of the box slips into two rabbets cut into each of the side pieces. The front is attached between the sides with a butt joint. The bottom is glued and nailed into place. Once cut to size, the sliding lid is either beveled or rabbeted to slide in and out of three grooves, which are cut in the candle box's two sides and back. Cut a thumb notch on the top and you're done.

Box First

The sizes and dimensions given here are based on my large box. If you'd like to build the small box, check out "Building the Small Box" on the previous page.

First, cut all your stock to size. Next, cut a $1/4$" by $1/2$" rabbet at one end of each of the two sides C. Then cut a $1/4$" × $1/4$" groove $3/8$" from the top on the back B and two sides C. Next, cut the bottom D to size. If you'd like to make a two-board bottom for the large box, feel free. Simply cut a shiplap joint to join the two bottom pieces.

Before assembly, finish-sand the interiors of all your parts. It's easier now than later. Now, glue and nail the back B, front A and bottom D into place, as shown in the photo on the next page.

Use your table saw to cut the rabbets on one end of the two sides. The rabbets hold the back in place.

Use your table saw to cut the grooves at the top of the two sides and at the top of the back. These grooves must be right on for the sliding lid to work properly.

Lid Last

Now, turn your attention to the lid. Measure and cut the lid F to size. Cut a 14° bevel on the lid's back and two sides using your table saw as shown below. Check the fit.

Now, cut the thumb notch on the front end of the lid E. The notch is perfectly sized for your thumb to pull the sliding lid in and out. If you're building a few of these boxes at one time, drill out the notch using a 35mm bit in your drill press. You'll need to make a jig, as shown on the next page. The thumb notch is drilled at a 15° angle, $\frac{1}{4}$" deep, with a $\frac{3}{8}$" offset from the back.

If you're building only one box, cut away the notch using a gouge and some sandpaper, as shown on the next page. Using a gouge also is a way to make your box look more authentic.

Before finishing, sand the exterior of the box and the lid. I fill in my tiny nail holes with wood putty. You can finish these boxes any way you like. I simply apply a couple of coats of lacquer, sanding between each coat.

Now that I build all our candle boxes, we really don't have an excuse to buy the boxes when scouting out antique shows. But that's OK. Not buying candle boxes simply has led to bigger and better finds.

Use the bottom piece as a place holder when nailing the front and back to the sides. It's easier to line everything up this way.

Tilt your saw blade 14° when cutting the bevel on the lid. If your lid is too small for this operation, simply cut rabbets to slide into the box's grooves.

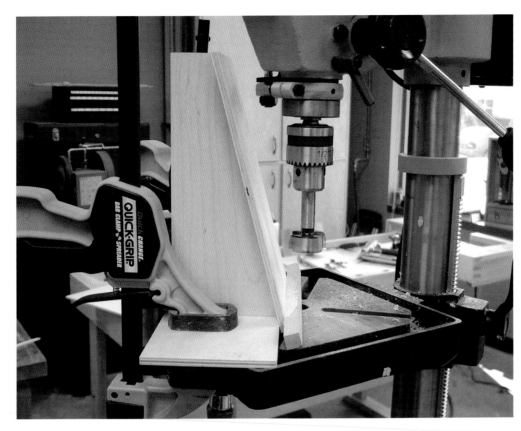

When building multiple boxes at one time (which I suggest), use your drill press and a 35mm bit to cut the thumb notch on the lid. Make a jig to cut the notch at a 15° angle, ¼" deep. I suggest doing a few practice runs first.

You can use a gouge to cut your thumb notch. Or cut the notch using your drill press, then clean up any burn marks with a gouge. Leave the tooling marks for an authentic look.

Country Hanging Cupboard

BY TROY SEXTON

I've built hundreds of single-door cabinets like this one. Some people use them as spice cabinets. Others use them in the bathroom as a medicine cabinet. You can hang them anywhere.

As I was building this particular cabinet, I realized that it would be an excellent project for beginners. It has all the traditional components of larger-scale cabinetry, yet it doesn't need a lot of material or tooling. Once you've built this cabinet, you can build something bigger using the same principles. Intermediate woodworkers might also pick up a trick or two because I build my cabinets just a bit differently.

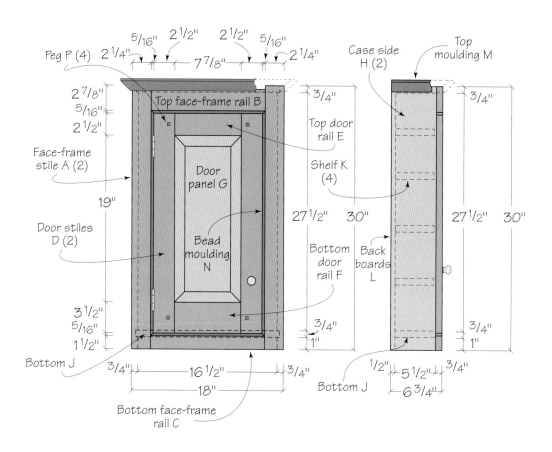

TOP MOULDING DETAIL

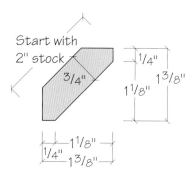

Start with 2" stock

3/4"

1/4"

1 3/8"

1 1/8"

1 1/8"

1/4"

1 3/8"

INCHES (MILLIMETERS)

REFERENCE	QUANTITY	PART	STOCK	THICKNESS	(mm)	WIDTH	(mm)	LENGTH	(mm)
A	2	face frame stiles	tiger maple	3/4	(19)	2 1/4	(57)	30	(762)
B	1	top face frame rail	tiger maple	3/4	(19)	2 7/8	(73)	15 1/2	(394)
C	1	bottom face frame rail	tiger maple	3/4	(19)	1 1/2	(38)	15 1/2	(394)
D	2	door stiles	tiger maple	3/4	(19)	2 1/2	(64)	25	(635)
E	1	top door rail	tiger maple	3/4	(19)	2 1/2	(64)	9 7/8	(251)
F	1	bottom door rail	tiger maple	3/4	(19)	3 1/2	(89)	9 7/8	(251)
G	1	door panel	tiger maple	5/8	(16)	8 3/8	(213)	19 1/2	(495)
H	2	case sides	tiger maple	3/4	(19)	6	(152)	30	(762)
J	2	top & bottom	tiger maple	3/4	(19)	5 1/2	(140)	17	(432)
K	4	shelves	tiger maple	3/4	(19)	5 7/16	(138)	16 7/16	(418)
L		back boards	tiger maple	1/2	(13)	17	(432)	30	(762)
M		top moulding	tiger maple	3/4	(19)	2	(51)	36	(914)
N		bead moulding	tiger maple	5/16	(8)	5/16	(8)	80	(2032)
P		pegs	tiger maple	5/16	(8)	5/16	(8)	1	(25)

hardware & supplies

2 hinges for door, Lee Valley Tools, #01H30.10

1 1 1/4" (32mm) brass knob w/ MSF (machine screw fitting), Horton Brasses, #K-12

Choose Your Wood

I used tiger maple for this project, but if this is your first cabinet, you might want to use poplar and then paint the finished item. Poplar is easy to work with and less expensive than maple, especially if the maple has some figure.

As in larger cabinets, most of the major components are made from $\frac{3}{4}$"-thick stock: the case sides, top, bottom, plus the rails and stiles for the door and the face frame. This cabinet has a solid-wood shiplapped back that's made from $\frac{1}{2}$"-thick pieces; the door panel is $\frac{5}{8}$" thick.

Face Frame: The Place to Start

It seems logical to begin by constructing the case. Don't. The size of your case and door are all determined by your face frame. Build it first and then you'll use your face frame to lay out your case and door. All face frames are made up of rails and stiles, much like a door. The stiles are the vertical pieces. The rails are the horizontal pieces that go between the stiles.

When you rip your stiles A to width on your table saw, make the rip $\frac{1}{16}$" wider than stated on the materials list. You need this extra width to overhang the sides of your case so you can trim it flush with a flush-cutting bit in a router. Once your pieces are cut to size, join the rails B and C and stiles A using mortise-and-tenon joints.

Begin by cutting the tenons on the rail ends. I know the books say to cut the mortise first, but I've found it's easier to lay out your mortises after your tenons are cut. Try it, and I think you'll agree.

The tenons should be $\frac{3}{8}$" thick (one-half as thick as your stock), centered on the rail and 1" long. I cut $\frac{1}{2}$" edge shoulders on the tenons. If they're any smaller, the mortise might blow out. Now, use your tenons to lay out your mortises on the stiles. Hold the tenon flat against the edge where the mortise will go and use the tenon like a ruler to mark your mortise.

Now, cut your mortises. Make all your mortises $1\frac{1}{16}$" deep, which will prevent your 1"-long tenons from bottoming out. You don't want your tenons to wobble in your mortises, yet you also don't want to have to beat the tenon in place.

Dry fit your face frame, then put glue on the mortise walls and clamp it up. While you're waiting for it to dry, turn your attention to the mitered bead moulding N that goes on all four inside edges of the face frames.

Years ago, I used to cut the beading into the rails and stiles. Then I would have to miter the bead and cut away the beading where the rails and stiles were joined. It sounds like a pain, and it was. Now I simply make my bead moulding separate from my face frame. Then I miter, nail and glue it in place. It looks just as good as what I used to do.

To make the bead moulding N, put a $\frac{1}{4}$" beading bit in your router and mount it in a router table. Then take a $\frac{3}{4}$"-thick board that's about 4" wide and cut the bead on one edge. Take that board to your table saw, set your rip fence to make a $\frac{3}{8}$"-wide cut and rip the bead from the wide board. Repeat this bead-moulding process three more times.

Now, take your strips and run them through your planer to reduce them in thickness to $\frac{5}{16}$". Miter the corners; then glue and nail them in place. Sand both sides of your face frame with 100-grit sandpaper and move on to building the door.

Adding this bead moulding to the inside of the face frame creates a nice shadow line around the door. Miter, glue and nail it in place. Don't forget to putty your nail holes.

Fit your door in the face frame before you attach the face frame to the case. Everything lays flat on your bench as you work. You'll find this procedure is a faster and easier way to get perfect results.

The Door

Why make the door next? For one thing, it is easier to hang your door in your face frame before you nail the face frame to your case.

I build my doors so they are the same size as my opening, then I shave off a little so there's a $^{1}/_{16}$" gap all around. This way if the door or face frame is out of square, I can taper the door edges to fit, hiding my error.

The door is built much like the face frame, using the same size mortises and tenons. The biggest difference is that you will need to cut a groove in your rails and stiles for the door panel, so your tenons must be haunched. A "haunch" is a little extra width in the tenon's shoulder. This extra width fills in the groove on the end of the stile.

Begin by cutting a $^{3}/_{8}$"-deep by $^{3}/_{8}$"-wide groove down the center of one long edge of your rails E and F and stiles D. Cut your tenons on your rails. Then cut your mortises on your stiles. Dry fit the pieces together and measure how big the center panel G should be.

You want the panel G to float to allow seasonal expansion and contraction, so cut the panel to allow $^{1}/_{8}$" expansion on either side. Now, raise the door panel G using your table saw or a cutter in your router table. Practice on scrap pieces of $^{5}/_{8}$" stock so you achieve the right lip, angle and fit.

When the panel G is complete, sand the raised section, then glue up the door. Be careful not to get any glue in the groove that holds the panel G. When the glue is dry, hang the door in your face frame.

Finally, the Case

The case is simple. The top and bottom J of the case fit into $^{1}/_{4}$"-deep dadoes and rabbets on the sides H. The back L rests in a rabbet on the sides H and is nailed to the back edge of the top and bottom J.

You'll use your face frame to lay out your joints on the sides H. You want the bottom J to end up $^{3}/_{16}$" higher than the top edge of the bottom face frame rail C. This allows your bottom J to act as a stop for the door. Mark the location of that $^{1}/_{4}$"-deep dado and cut. The top J rests in a $^{1}/_{4}$"-deep by $^{3}/_{4}$"-wide rabbet on the sides, cut using your table saw. Cut the $^{1}/_{2}$"-deep by $^{1}/_{4}$"-wide rabbet on the back edge of the sides H.

Drill holes for shelf pins and space them 1" apart on the sides H. Sand the inside of the case. You'll notice that the top and bottom J are $^{1}/_{2}$" narrower than the sides H. This is to give you a good place to nail the back pieces L to the case. Now, assemble the case using glue and nails, making sure the top, bottom and sides are all flush at the front sides of the cabinet.

Attach the face frame to the case using glue and nails. Now, trim the face frame flush to the case using a bearing-guided flush-cutting bit in your router. Finish-sand the cabinet to 180 grit.

Take your scrap pieces and use them to make a shiplapped back. Cut a $^{1}/_{4}$" × $^{1}/_{2}$" rabbet on the edges and then cut a bead on one edge using a $^{1}/_{4}$" beading bit in your router table. You want to give the back pieces L room to expand and contract; about $^{1}/_{8}$" between each board should be fine.

Cut the moulding M for the top so it resembles the drawing detail on page 56. Finish-sand everything, then nail the moulding M to the top J.

I like to peg the tenons in my doors to add a little strength. Drill a $^{1}/_{4}$"-diameter hole most of the way through the stile and tenon. To make each peg P, whittle a square piece of stock so it's round on one end, put glue in the hole and pound it in place. Cut the peg P nearly flush. You want it to be a little proud of the stile; it's a traditional touch.

Now, break all the edges of the case with 120-grit sandpaper and putty all your nail holes. Paint, dye or stain all the components (I used a water-based aniline dye). Then add two coats of clear finish and nail the back pieces L in place. Hang the cabinet by screwing through the back boards into a stud in your wall.

Here you can see how the bottom of the case acts as a door stop. This is one of the reasons I build my face frames first: I can make sure my bottom will be in perfect position.

Curly Maple Country Wall Shelf

BY STEVE SHANESY

Country furniture is currently popular for many reasons. It not only reminds us of simpler times, but its casual elegance helps produce a friendly, informal setting where we can relax and retreat from the hustle and bustle of our busy, modern world. But these country-inspired styles hold additional appeal for the woodworker, especially those of us with limited time and machines, because like their original antique cousins, country pieces are relatively simple to build with basic tools.

Country woodworkers of the Colonial era might have been itinerant tradesmen moving from town to town. Because they were working for clients with less money, the country woodworker combined simple joinery and a modest assortment of tools to build plain furniture for his clientele. Although I used a table saw and router in constructing this wall-hung shelf, it's not difficult to imagine doing all the work with a hand crosscut saw and ripsaw, a chisel or two, and a couple of basic hand planes.

With a nod to the past, I included an element or two that puts this project in the antique reproduction category. I used cut nails, and not only did I dovetail the top rail and drawers, but I used a bevel-edge drawer bottom, as well.

Here's the assembled dovetail on the top rail joining the case side. The top edge, hidden by the crown, was not dovetailed but simply nailed to the side.

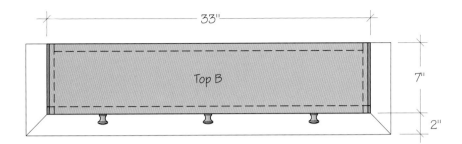

33"

Top B

7"

2"

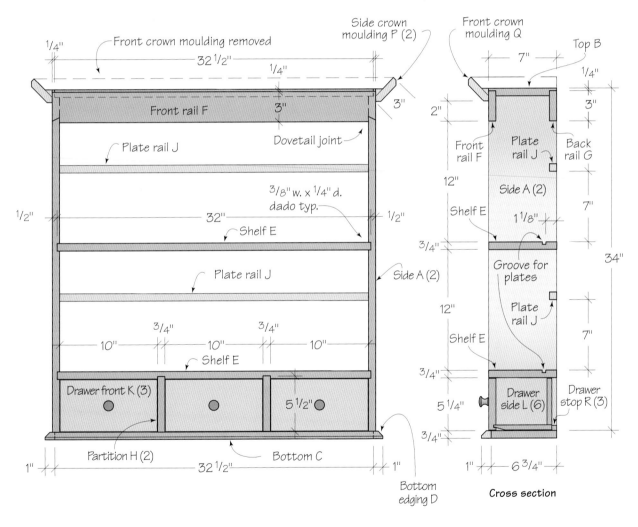

Front crown moulding removed

Side crown moulding P (2)

Front crown moulding Q

Top B

1/4"

32 1/2"

1/4"

7"

1/4"

Front rail F

3"

3"

3"

Dovetail joint

Plate rail J

Plate rail J

Back rail G

2"

Front rail F

12"

3/8" w. x 1/4" d. dado typ.

Side A (2)

Shelf E

7"

1/2"

32"

1/2"

Shelf E

Side A (2)

1 1/8"

3/4"

Plate rail J

Groove for plates

34"

12"

Plate rail J

Shelf E

7"

10"

3/4"

10"

3/4"

10"

Shelf E

Drawer front K (3)

5 1/2"

3/4"

Shelf E

5 1/4"

Drawer side L (6)

Drawer stop R (3)

Partition H (2)

Bottom C

3/4"

1"

32 1/2"

1"

1"

6 3/4"

1"

Bottom edging D

Cross section

REFERENCE	QUANTITY	PART	STOCK	THICKNESS	(mm)	WIDTH	(mm)	LENGTH	(mm)	COMMENTS
A	2	sides	P	3/4	(19)	7	(178)	34	(864)	rabbet top edge, dado for shelves
B	1	top	P	3/4	(19)	7	(178)	32 1/2	(826)	rabbet two long edges
C	1	bottom	S	3/4	(19)	7	(178)	32 1/2	(826)	
D	1	bottom edging	P	3/4	(19)	1	(25)	48	(1219)	cut edging to fit the bottom ends and front edge
E	2	shelves	P	3/4	(19)	7	(178)	32	(813)	run plate grooves before assembly, dado bottom shelf for drawer partitions
F	1	front rail	P	3/4	(19)	3	(76)	33	(838)	half dovetail to sides
G	1	back rail	P	3/4	(19)	3	(76)	31 1/2	(800)	
H	2	partitions	P	3/4	(19)	5 1/2	(140)	7	(178)	
J	2	plate rails	P	3/4	(19)	3/4	(19)	31 1/2	(800)	
K	3	drawer fronts	P	3/4	(19)	5 1/4	(133)	10	(254)	
L	6	drawer sides	S	1/2	(13)	5 1/4	(133)	6 1/8	(156)	
M	3	drawer backs	S	1/2	(13)	4 11/16	(119)	10	(254)	
N	3	drawer bottoms	S	1/2	(13)	6	(152)	9 3/8	(238)	
P	2	side crown mouldings	P	3/4	(19)	3	(76)	9	(229)	
Q	1	front crown moulding	P	3/4	(19)	3	(76)	36 3/4	(934)	
R	3	drawer stops	S	1/2	(13)	1/2	(13)	10	(254)	

P = Primary (figured maple, cherry or poplar); S = Secondary

hardware & supplies

3 1" (25mm) diameter wood pulls cut nails

Prepare the Stock

Although it's expensive, I selected curly maple, because little wood is required for the project. Cherry or even poplar would also be good choices. Because figured woods such as curly, fiddleback or tiger maple are expensive, I mixed in regular maple in the places where the wood really wouldn't be seen. I also used a less-expensive secondary wood for my drawer sides, back and bottom.

Before starting in the shop, I made up my materials list. I always begin with an accurate, detailed list, which was especially helpful in laying out the cutting of the three curly maple boards from which I had to get all my pieces. I was able to plan where the best figure would be showcased in the project and make sure grain direction was balanced and pleasing to the eye.

Because the maple I bought was already surfaced to 3/4", the only rough preparation required was to straighten the edges on the jointer. I then cut all my pieces to width and length according to my materials list. I did, however, put off cutting the crown molding miters and drawer fronts until the case was assembled. As with all projects, cut similar parts on the same setups to maintain consistency and accuracy. Just remember that you'll have rights and lefts, ups and downs, as you proceed through your cutting.

Mill the Joints

Before leaving the table saw, I cut my 3/4" by 1/2"-deep rabbets on the top ends of the two sides A and on the long edges of the top B, using a dado set. I then made my 3/4" by 1/4"-deep dado cuts in the sides A (to hold the two shelves E) and on the bottom side of the lower shelf F (to house the two verticals that form the partitions between the three drawers).

Before assembly, I routed a plate groove on each shelf E top surface and hand cut the dovetails and pins for the top front rail F where it joins the sides A (the back rail G butts to the sides A and is nailed in place). Because the front rail F extends to the top rabbet, only the bottom half of the dovetail required cutting.

Part of my stinginess with the curly maple included making the bottom C from regular maple, which I edged with 1"-wide by 3/4"-thick curly maple. An added benefit was that no end grain showed on the bottom C, and the curly grain is especially striking with the bevel detail on the sides and front. When gluing the edges, a spline or biscuit is required for the end grain of the bottom but unnecessary for joining the long grain to long grain on the front edge. It's important to rout the bevel detail before assembly.

Assemble the Case

Unless you want to hold parts in place while assembling, clamps are not required, because all joints are nailed using the antique-looking square cut nails. In fact, you could make a case for eliminating glue, as well, but gluing is an old habit of mine that's just too hard to break.

First, assemble the lower shelf E and drawer partitions H. Because these are nailed from the top down, it's easier to swing a hammer now rather than when it's assembled with the sides and upper shelf. The cut nails are anything but delicate and, with their wedged shape, are prime candidates for causing splits. I overcame this potential hazard by drilling a pilot hole for each nail. It's also important to consider a nice spacing arrangement for the nails, rather than just accepting arbitrary, approximate locations. (Just because you're using nails doesn't mean it's not furniture!)

The sides A, shelves E and top B came next. Each was set in its dado or rabbet and nailed. I then attached the front top rail F in its dovetail and nailed it where it sits in the rabbet of the top B. I likewise nailed the back rail G in its rabbet, and also nailed it through the side. With this complete, I was then able to turn the piece upside down to set the bottom C in place and nail it. I used two nails each for the sides A and drawer partitions H. Again, I drilled pilot holes for each nail. Finally, I glued the drawer stops R in place.

Make and Attach the Crown

Everything having to do with the crown moulding P and Q was done on the table saw. Its shape was made by simply making two 45° angle cuts, one for the bottom and one for the top. Before cutting, however, I laid out the profile of the crown and quickly concluded that an extra triangular-shaped piece would be needed on the back side to create a sufficient flat to nail it easily to the case. This was accomplished simply enough by cutting an equilateral triangle with ³⁄₄" legs. The triangular-shaped piece was glued (not nailed) in place so

Before assembly, the plain maple bottom is edged with curly maple, then chamfered using a router.

that it lined up with the angle cut on the bottom edge. (See the crown moulding detail drawing on the following page.)

After cutting the angles on the long edges of the board (giving the crown its final profile), I cut the compound miters where the sides of the crown meet their corresponding front. This was accomplished easily enough on the table saw by setting the blade to a 30° angle and the slot miter gauge to 35° (see the picture on the following page). With careful measurements and thoroughly thinking through the cuts (I had to be careful; I was working with the last piece of curly maple in the shop!), the crown parts were complete. To attach the crown to the case, I nailed the parts on with the bottom of the crown 1" down from the top of the case.

To pull the compound miter joint together, I used a few pieces of masking tape (as shown on the following page). This technique was much faster and simpler than cutting clamping cauls to just the right shape, which would be an absolute requirement if one were to use clamps to do the job.

Cut and Assemble the Drawer Parts

All three drawers are the same size. The curly maple fronts K were cut from the same board and kept in sequence so that the grain matched across. The sizes provided in the materials list are for ¹⁄₂" sides L, backs M and bottoms N with ³⁄₄" fronts K. I used half-blind dovetails for joining the sides L to the front K and back M. If you use a different construction method, your sizes will change, except for the drawer openings.

I used a Porter-Cable dovetail jig outfitted with a template for making ¹⁄₂" dovetails and box joints. Although these, and most other jigs take some precise setup, they produce nice, repeatable results. For this project, I would have preferred Porter-Cable's template that makes 2" dovetails because these would have given a more "hand-cut" look. But as is, I'm satisfied with the look achieved using the ¹⁄₂" template.

The drawer bottoms N were made in the traditional style of a bevel-edged panel. The bevel is cut in the same manner as raised panels on the table saw. Simply tilt the blade to about 15° and run the panels on edge. Calculate the fence setting so that the bevel you make fits nicely into a $\frac{1}{4}$" × $\frac{1}{4}$" groove that starts $\frac{1}{4}$" from the bottom edge of the drawer sides L and front K. Using half-blind dovetails required me to make a stopped dado for the drawer bottom groove in the drawer front. To mill the dado, I used a router set up on the router table with a $\frac{1}{4}$" straight bit. I trimmed the back M so that its width is $\frac{1}{2}$" narrower than the sides L, which allows the bottom N to slip in from behind. The drawers are small enough to slip simply in and out of their openings with no guide system required. For pulls, I purchased turned round knobs at the local hardware store.

The crown compound miter is cut on the table saw. Tilt the blade to 30° and the miter gauge to 35°.

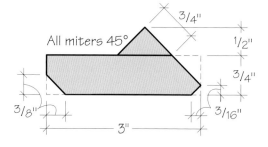

A simple method for "clamping" the crown when gluing is to use masking tape; just pull it tight over the joint.

Drawer sides were joined to the front and back using $\frac{1}{2}$" half-blind dovetails cut on a dovetail jig.

Finishing

Because the parts were presanded to 120 grit before assembly, I picked up the sanding chore using 150 grit with the random-orbit palm sander. I proceeded to 220 grit and finished sanding by breaking all the sharp edges with 120-grit sandpaper.

Because I wanted the shelf to look as if it was already a number of years old, I mixed brown and yellow aniline dye stain to give it a honey color, the approximate color a shellac finish on maple might attain after years of exposure to light. To avoid the splotchiness of maple and stain, I sprayed the aniline dye stain and immediately wiped it down with lacquer thinner on a clean rag. This evened the color for good consistency.

I topped the color with a water-based lacquer that I sprayed on. After the first coat dried for 45 minutes, I sanded it with 360-grit paper, then sprayed a second wet coat. It dried to a smooth finish. To create a little contrast, I sprayed the pulls with black lacquer from an aerosol can and then topped them with a coat of clear lacquer.

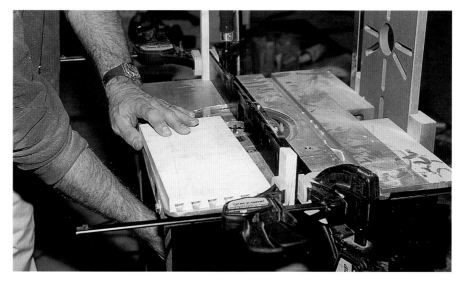

A stopped groove was required on the inside of the drawer front to receive the bottom. It was cut with a router.

The drawer bottoms are $1/2$" thick but are beveled to slip into a $1/4$" groove, a traditional drawer construction method.

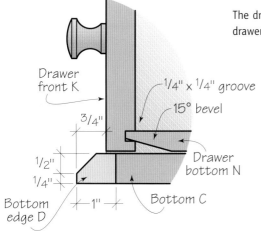

BOTTOM DETAIL

Drawer front K

$1/4$" x $1/4$" groove

15° bevel

$3/4$"

$1/2$"

$1/4$"

Drawer bottom N

Bottom edge D

1"

Bottom C

Mantle Clock

BY DAVID THIEL

You might not be ready to build your own sideboard, but you can start your Craftsman collection with this simple clock. The only tough part of the project is finding a great piece of quarter-sawn white oak (1" × 6" × 96").

First Things First

Cut the pieces according to the materials list. Resaw and bookmatch the front for an impressive appearance. Taper the front A to an 8" width at the top. Then, crosscut a 45° angle on the top and bottom edges of both sides D, parallel to one another.

Cut the Front

Cut the dial hole and pendulum slots in the front A. Use a chamfer bit to cut the angle profile in the dial hole.

Cut the Top and Bottom

To cut the top C and bottom B chamfer details (including the $^{1}/_{8}$" bead), use your table saw. Start by making a $^{1}/_{8}$"-deep cut 1" in on the ends and front edges. Cut the bevel by running the pieces on edge (use a zero-clearance throat plate) with the blade set to 23°. Set the blade height to intersect with the bead cut and set the fence to leave the $^{3}/_{16}$" flat. To inset the front A $^{1}/_{4}$" back from the sides D, lay it on a $^{1}/_{4}$" piece of fiberboard as a spacer; glue the two sides D to the front A. The falloff pieces from the front taper make

INCHES (MILLIMETERS)

REFERENCE	QUANTITY	PART	STOCK	THICKNESS	(mm)	WIDTH	(mm)	LENGTH	(mm)
A	1	front	white oak	1/2	(13)	9	(229)	14	(356)
B	1	bottom	white oak	3/4	(19)	5	(127)	12	(305)
C	1	top	white oak	3/4	(19)	5	(127)	10	(254)
D	2	sides	white oak	1/2	(13)	$3^{15}/_{16}$	(100)	$14^1/_8$	(359)
E	1	back	oak plywood	1/4	(6)	$9^7/_8$	(251)	$14^9/_{16}$	(370)
F	1	dial support block	pine	3/4	(19)	$5^1/_2$	(140)	6	(152)
G	4	fake through-tenons	white oak	1/4	(6)	1/2	(13)	$1^1/_2$	(38)
H	8	fake pins	white oak	1/8	(3)	1/4	(6)	1/4	(6)

hardware & supplies

1 clock mechanism, Woodcraft #142321–142325 (your choice)
1 clock face, Woodcraft #124895
No. 4 x 3/4" (19mm) brass screws

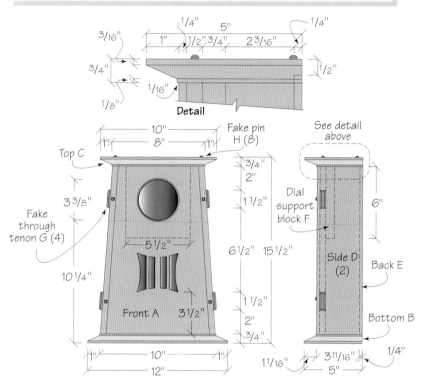

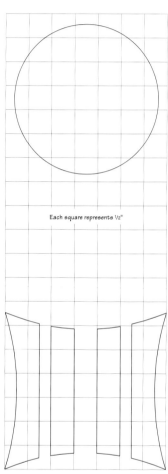

Each square represents 1/2"

ENLARGE 200% FOR FULL-SIZED PATTERN

perfect clamping cauls to exert equal pressure on the sides D. Drill pilot holes, then nail the bottom B and top C to the sides D, leaving a $^1/_{16}$" setback. Set the nails.

Through-Tenons

Cut, chamfer, then glue the fake through-tenons G as shown on the drawing. Cut, chamfer and glue the fake pins H to cover the nail holes. Rout a $^1/_4$" by $^3/_8$"-deep rabbet in the clock's back edges. Then fit the back E into the rabbet.

The Block and Face

Cut the dial support block F and glue the clock face to the block, centered and $2^1/_2$" down from the top of the block. Apply two coats of clear finish to the block and face, which is typically paper.

Attach the Hands

Drill a hole in the center of the clock face for attaching the hands to the clock mechanism and attach the movement to the back of the support block F.

Apply Glaze and Finish

To finish, first apply warm brown glaze to the clock case. Apply a few coats of clear finish.

Last Things Last

Screw the dial support block F to the inside of the face. Shorten and attach the pendulum, then drill pilot holes into the back E and attach using No. 4 × $^3/_4$" brass screws.

Basic Bookcases

BY DAVID THIEL

When it comes to furniture projects, there isn't an easier place to start than bookcases. They're simple boxes with no drawers, no doors and straightforward joinery. As far as practical, you'll be amazed as to what can be stored in them.

A $^3/_8$" × $^3/_8$" through-rabbet runs on the inside back edge of all the sides. A stopped rabbet runs on the inside back edge of each top.

Use a template to locate the shelf pins, which are drilled to provide equal spaces. Drill extra holes 1" up and 1" down from the equidistant holes for adjustable spacing.

You can finish these bookcases with a few coats of a clear satin lacquer. But if natural color or lacquer isn't your first choice, you can choose any number of stain options or clear topcoats.

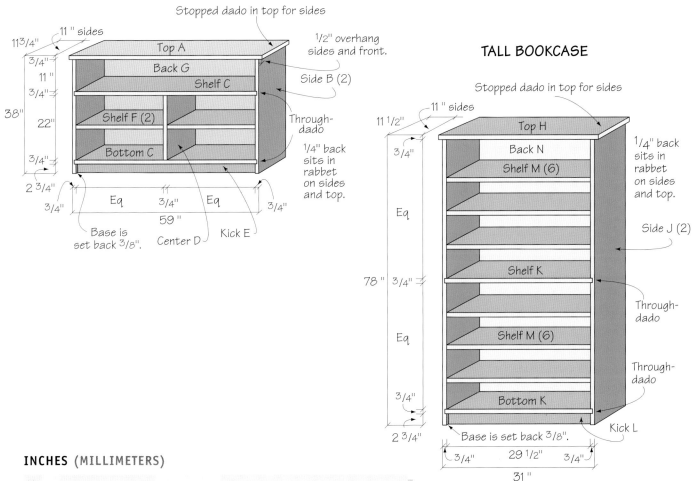

LOW BOOKCASE

Stopped dado in top for sides

11 3/4"
11 " sides
3/4"
11 "
3/4"
38"
22"
3/4"
2 3/4"
3/4"

Top A

Back G

Shelf C

Shelf F (2)

Bottom C

Eq   11   Eq
3/4"   3/4"
59 "   3/4"

Base is
set back 3/8".

Center D

Kick E

1/2" overhang
sides and front.

Side B (2)

Through-
dado

1/4" back
sits in
rabbet
on sides
and top.

TALL BOOKCASE

Stopped dado in top for sides

11 1/2"
11 " sides
3/4"
Eq
78 "
3/4"
Eq
3/4"
2 3/4"

Top H

Back N

Shelf M (6)

Shelf K

Shelf M (6)

Bottom K

3/4"   29 1/2"   3/4"
31 "

Base is set back 3/8".

1/4" back
sits in
rabbet
on sides
and top.

Side J (2)

Through-
dado

Through-
dado

Kick L

INCHES (MILLIMETERS)

REFERENCE	QUANTITY	PART	STOCK	THICKNESS	(mm)	WIDTH	(mm)	LENGTH	(mm)
LOW BOOKCASE									
A	1	top	solid oak	3/4	(19)	11 1/2	(292)	60	(1524)
B	2	sides	solid oak	3/4	(19)	11	(279)	37 5/8	(956)
C	2	bottom/shelf	solid oak	3/4	(19)	10 5/8	(270)	58 1/4	(1480)
D	1	center	solid oak	3/4	(19)	10 5/8	(270)	22 3/4	(578)
E	1	kick	solid oak	3/4	(19)	2 3/4	(70)	57 1/2	(1461)
F	2	shelves	solid oak	3/4	(19)	10 1/2	(267)	28 3/8	(721)
G	1	back	oak plywood	1/4	(6)	34 7/8	(886)	58 1/4	(1480)
TALL BOOKCASE									
H	1	top	solid oak	3/4	(19)	11 1/2	(292)	32	(813)
J	2	sides	solid oak	3/4	(19)	11	(279)	77 5/8	(1972)
K	2	bottom/shelf	solid oak	3/4	(19)	10 5/8	(270)	30 1/4	(768)
L	1	kick	solid oak	3/4	(19)	2 3/4	(70)	29 1/2	(749)
M	6	shelves	solid oak	3/4	(19)	10 1/2	(267)	29 1/2	(749)
N	1	back	oak plywood	1/4	(6)	30 1/4	(768)	74 7/8	(1902)

Heirloom Photo Album

BY STEVE SHANESY

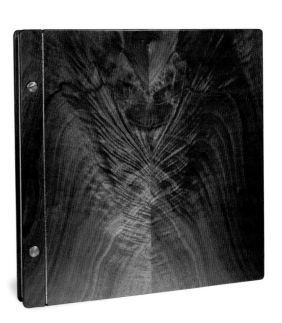

Given the current craze for scrapbooking, I thought it high time we woodworkers weigh in with our own version of what a memorable photo album should look like.

And if you are tempted to rip out these magazine pages before your spouse sees them and places an order for, say, a dozen or so, fear not. This truly is an easy project. It could even be simpler than what you see here if you skip the resawing and bookmatching of the $\frac{1}{4}$"-thick front and back covers.

In fact, if you made five or six at a time, you could probably spend no more than a half hour on each one. Or you could go in the other direction and make it more complicated with inlay or chip carving on the front.

There could, in fact, be many variations on this project. You could easily alter the size of the covers for smaller photo album sheets, or you could set it up with blank pages for use as a personal journal or documents from your family tree research.

No matter what direction your version of this project takes, two simple elements will make it all possible: the post binding screws that fix the covers and pages together, and the small-scale continuous hinge that allows the covers

to open, making them truly functional. The hinges and post binding screws can be ordered through the Lee Valley Tools woodworking catalog.

Getting Started

A trip to an art or office-supply store is the first step. Select the photo page size you want to work with. Some pages simply are plain sheets that are inserted in clear plastic sheet protectors. The protectors, in turn, are usually punched for use in a three-ring binder. The sheets I used were hole-punched for post binding and "hinged," meaning each sheet was made to fold at a given place along the edge where it would be bound into the album.

I selected a sheet size that was 12" × 12". Next, I ordered my post binding screws and hinge from Lee Valley. The screws, called Chicago Bolts in the catalog, come in various lengths, with each length allowing for a $\frac{1}{4}$" adjustment. The brass hinge comes in a 3' length and is easily cut.

The page size and hinge gave me dimensions I could start to work with. The wood covers' finished size is $\frac{1}{4}$" × $12\frac{1}{2}$" square. This allows $\frac{1}{4}$" for the cover to overlap top and bottom. The bound side has $\frac{1}{8}$" overlap, leaving $\frac{3}{8}$"

for the open side. When I cut the pieces, I made the width $12\frac{5}{8}$". This allowed a table saw cut to separate the binding strip from the cover piece. The cover thickness was $\frac{1}{4}$", which is perfect for the hinge leaf.

A Word about Wood Choice

My album covers are made using feather-figured walnut that was resawn and bookmatched. It came from a tree in my neighborhood that was taken down and sawn into lumber about three years ago. Although it's been air drying all this time, I was nervous as a cat about my pieces warping after resawing and glue-up. Highly figured wood often has a mind of its own. I know that walnut is a relatively stable wood, like mahogany, but I kept my pieces on a flat surface with a weight on top until I was able to put a finish on them. Even at the thin $\frac{1}{4}$" dimension, I was lucky and both pieces have remained perfectly flat.

The point of all this is to remind you to be cautious about your wood selection and handling. Try to use a stable species. A narrower album would be less risky.

Hardware Installation and Finishing

I followed the hole patterns for the post binding screws that were already in the album sheets. Allowing for the top and bottom overhang, my hole center for the screws was $2\frac{9}{16}$" from the top and bottom. From the binding edge, I marked a hole center of $\frac{1}{2}$".

The posts required a $\frac{1}{4}$" hole with a $\frac{1}{2}$"-diameter counterbore to recess the

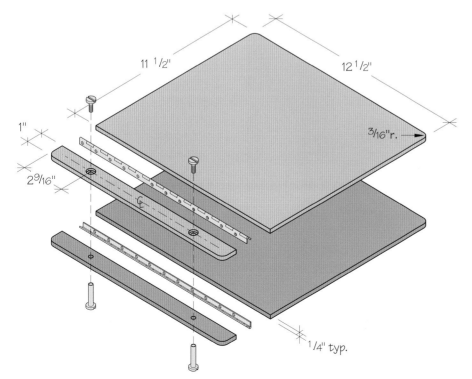

11 $\frac{1}{2}$"   12 $\frac{1}{2}$" $\frac{3}{16}$"r.

1" $2\frac{9}{16}$" $\frac{1}{4}$" typ.

hardware & supplies

1   12mm x 800mm brass piano hinge, Lee Valley Tools #00D50

    13mm brass escutcheon pins, flathead, Lee Valley Tools, #00D41

    4 pack 30–36mm Chicago brass bolts, Lee Valley Tools, #00K40.05

    Masters Magic Sanding Sealer, aerosol can, Craft Suppliers USA, #299-0100

    Masters Magic Satin Spray Lacquer, aerosol can, Craft Suppliers USA, #299-0001

Brass miniature continuous hinges are a cinch to cut with a pair of metal shears. Make your cut at the joint where two hinge leaves meet nearest your ideal length.

An ordinary paper hole punch enlarged the holes that were prepunched by the manufacturer of the photo album sheets.

flat heads of the screws. I used a Forstner bit for drilling in my drill press. It is necessary to drill the front and back banding strip exactly alike.

At this point I progressively sanded to 220 grit, rounded the outside corners to a $^3/_{16}$" radius, and heavily eased the edges, except for the edges where the hinge would be installed.

The finish may be a bit more complicated than you are accustomed to, but the fantastic figure in the walnut demanded as good a finish as I know how to do. And it was worth each step. Be-

cause walnut is an open-pore wood, I filled the grain using paste wood filler. I added oil-based walnut stain to the filler to color the filler and the wood. After applying the filler, I allowed it to dry for 24 hours.

For a clear top coat I used a lacquer that comes in an aerosol spray can. The product is the best lacquer in a can I've ever used. It's called Master's Magic and is available from Craft Suppliers USA, the Woodturners Catalog. A can of sanding sealer and satin finish lacquer are required, and the product should be used only in a well-ventilated area free of open flames (including pilot lights on water heaters or furnaces) or potential sparks.

After applying the sanding sealer, carefully sand with 360-grit paper, being especially careful near the edges. The idea is to lightly sand down any dust particles or bubbles that may have formed but not to sand into the stain color below the sealer. After sanding the sealer, spray two top coats with the satin finish. Allow the finish to cure overnight, even though it will be dry to the touch in 15 minutes.

I used a pair of snips to cut the hinges to $12^1/_8$" long. Cut the hinge at one of the leaf joints. The hinges are attached using flathead brads that you should order along with the hinges. Predrill the holes for the brads into the edge of the wood, leaving about $^1/_4$" of the brad length not drilled. Predrilling should ensure nothing pokes though the face of the cover.

Insert the post part of the post binding screws and fill your photo page inserts. I found that it was necessary to slightly enlarge the holes in the sheets with an ordinary paper punch. When done, lay the other cover over the post and then insert the screw.

If you are considering leaving the album on a coffee table or if you just want to protect the back cover from scratches, put a felt bumper pad in each corner of the back cover.

As a photo album or scrapbook, this project makes an extra special gift for an extra special occasion. Is there a family wedding in your future?

Versailles Tub With Obelisk Top

BY RICHARD BLIZZARD

One of the basic methods of joining lumber together has always been the mortise-and-tenon joint.
This joint, however, is quite difficult for a novice to
master and requires access to a number of rather
specialized tools. Therefore, the challenge for me
was to design a box structure that was free from
traditional joints, but still had sufficient strength to
do the job. The obelisk top requires a degree of
patience to build well; you also need a jig to assemble it on — but more on that later.

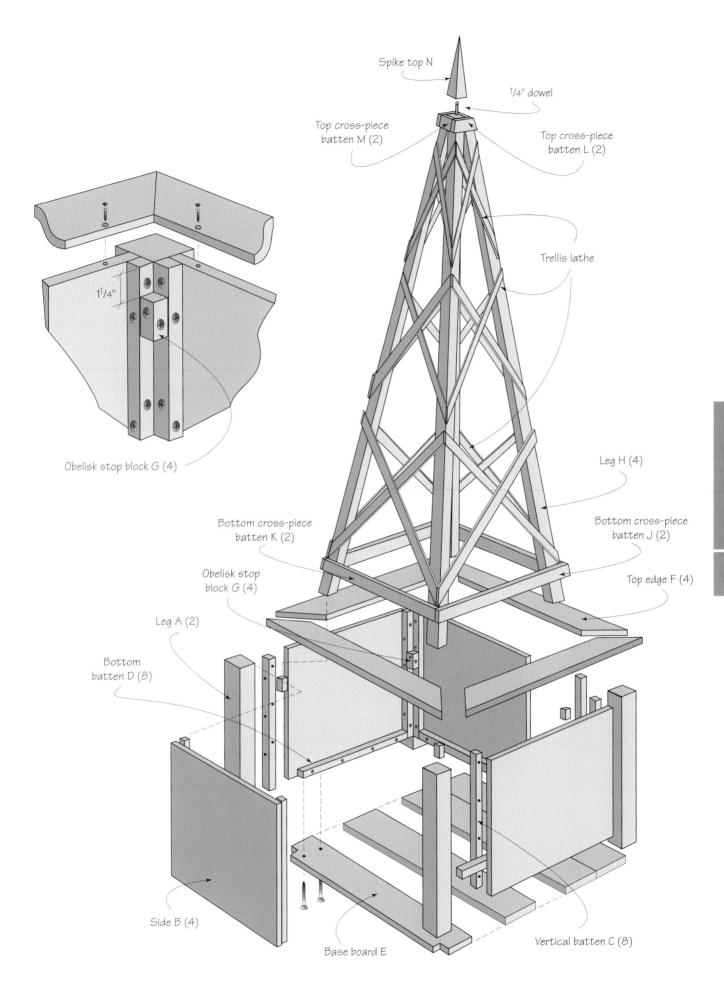

Spike top N

¹/₄" dowel

Top cross-piece batten M (2)

Top cross-piece batten L (2)

Trellis lathe

1¹/₄"

Leg H (4)

Obelisk stop block G (4)

Bottom cross-piece batten K (2)

Bottom cross-piece batten J (2)

Obelisk stop block G (4)

Top edge F (4)

Leg A (2)

Bottom batten D (8)

Side B (4)

Base board E

Vertical batten C (8)

REFERENCE	QUANTITY	PART	STOCK	THICKNESS	(mm)	WIDTH	(mm)	LENGTH	(mm)	COMMENTS
PLANTER BOX										
A	4	legs	treated lumber	1½	(38)	1½	(38)	19	(483)	Purchase 2x2 lumber
B	4	sides	exterior grade	¾	(19)	16	(406)	16	(406)	
C	8	vertical cleats	treated lumber	¾	(19)	¾	(19)	15	(381)	Purchase 1x1 lumber
D	8	top & bottom cleats	treated lumber	¾	(19)	¾	(19)	14¼	(362)	Purchase 1x1 lumber
E	4	base boards	treated lumber	¾	(19)	5½	(114)	17½	(445)	Purchase 1x6 lumber
F	4	top edge boards	treated lumber	¾	(19)	3½	(89)	22¼	(565)	Purchase 1x4 lumber
G	4	obelisk stop blocks	treated lumber	¾	(19)	¾	(19)	3	(76)	Purchase 1x1 lumber
OBELISK TOP										
H	4	legs	treated lumber	1½	(38)	1½	(38)	60¼	(1530)	Purchase 2x2 lumber
J	2	bottom battens	treated lumber	¾	(19)	1½	(38)	17	(432)	Purchase 1x2 lumber
K	2	bottom battens	treated lumber	¾	(19)	1½	(38)	15	(381)	Purchase 1x2 lumber
L	2	top battens	treated lumber	¾	(19)	1½	(38)	4⅞	(89)	Purchase 1x2 lumber
M	2	top battens	treated lumber	¾	(19)	1½	(38)	3⅜	(51)	Purchase 1x2 lumber
N	1	spiked top	treated lumber	1½	(38)	1½	(38)	6½	(165)	Scrap 2x2 lumber

hardware & supplies

1 ¼" dia. (6mm) dowel rod

1 ¼" dia. (6mm) dowel rod

1 bundle ¼"-thick (6mm) trellis lathe

1¾" (45mm) zinc-plated deck screws

1¼" (32mm) zinc-plated deck screws

exterior glue

exterior paint

Planter Box

1 Cut the four legs A of the box to length.

2 Cut the vertical cleats C and attach them to the two inside faces of each of the legs A using glue and screws. The tops of the cleats and the tops of the legs are flush.

3 Cut the sides B to size.

4 Now, glue and screw the sides B to the cleats C, as shown in the diagram. Keep the top of the sides B flush with the tops of the leg A. Once all four sides B are screwed in place, a bottomless box is formed.

5 Screw cleats D 1" up from the bottom edges of the plywood sides B. Use at least four screws per cleat because the whole weight of the soil that fills the box will rest on these cleats.

6 The base E is made from individual boards. Because the legs A protrude into the inner corners of the box, you have to cut out two small notches in each of the two end boards E to fit them around the legs. Mark the notches and cut them with a handsaw.

7 Turn the box upside down and install the base boards E.

8 Screw the base securely to the bottom cleats D around the bottom edges. Now, bore holes at random to allow for drainage; these holes need to be fairly large — at least ½".

9 Now, turn your attention to the top of the box, which wants strips to cap it off. Although it is not essential, these look really nice when cut to 45° miters at the corners. The alternative is to retain straight edges on the top boards and simply butt them up.

Before you attach the top edges F to the legs A, as shown in the diagram, you need to screw the top battens D in place around the top edges of the box. This process is really a repeat of the job you did for the base in step 5.

10 Using glue and screws, attach the four obelisk stop blocks G to the inside corners of the planter box. Locate them as shown in the illustration.

BEVEL CUTS ON PLYWOOD EDGES

Be careful when cutting and handling plywood after you've cut bevels on the edges. Plywood edges are fragile and can be easily chipped or nicked. Also, I've received some nasty cuts from these edges as they are sharp!

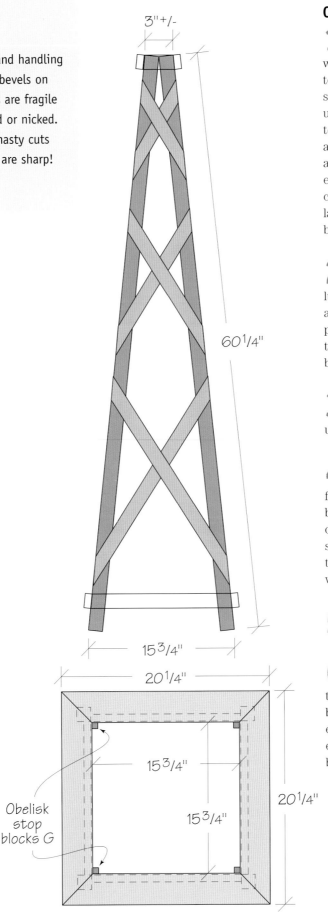

3"+/-

60¹/4"

15³/4"

20¹/4"

15³/4"

15³/4"

20¹/4"

Obelisk stop blocks G

Obelisk Top

1 Using the illustration on page 75 as a guide, lay two legs H on a flat work surface and attach a bottom batten K and a top batten L using glue and screws. Then, attach the trellis lathe using glue and screws. The easiest way to attach the lathe is simply lay a strip at an angle as shown in the illustration and screw it in place. Then trim the ends flush to the legs using a hand crosscut saw. Repeat this for all the lathe strips. Make two of these assemblies.

2 Lay the two trellis assemblies on edge so they look similar to the illustration on this page. Glue and screw a top batten L and a bottom batten J in place. Flip this assembly over and attach the remaining top batten L and a bottom batten J.

3 Attach the trellis lathe to the two sides of the assembled obelisk using the same method as in step 1.

4 Now, make a spiked top N. This is purely a matter of choice; you can fit a ball top if you wish. The spike can be made from a scrap 2×2. Drill a ¹/4"-diameter hole in the bottom of the spike and in the top of the obelisk. Attach the spike to the top of the obelisk with glue and a ¹/4" × 2" dowel.

5 Use a protective wood-care product or paint to finish.

6 When you install the obelisk assembly into the planter box, set the ends of the legs on the obelisk stop blocks. You may want to toe screw the ends of the legs to the stop blocks to ensure the obelisk doesn't get toppled by the wind.

Three-Legged Shop Stool

BY JIM STACK

I've made a lot of shop stools throughout the years, and I always wanted one that I could sit on without having to shift the stool or walk around it until I "lined up" with the seat. A three-cornered stool was a logical choice because it's easier to straddle a corner when plopping down.

I wanted to make the stool seat out of solid wood, which presented a problem with grain configuration. In order to get maximum strength for the wedged tenons at the tops of the legs, the wedges needed to run at a right angle to the grain in the seat. If I used a solid chunk of wood for the seat, only one leg would have the proper orientation for the wedge to do its job. The other two legs would end up having the wedges running almost parallel to the seat grain (see illustration on the next page).

I decided to make the seat using three separate pieces of wood with the grain running toward the center of the seat. The next question was how to join the three pieces to create a joint that would not break under pressure. I tried biscuits first. They made a strong joint but the individual pieces had grain movement that opened the joints up. No good.

After considering some other options (lap and tongue-and-groove joints), I decided that cross-grained splines would keep the joints tight and still permit the wood pieces to move.

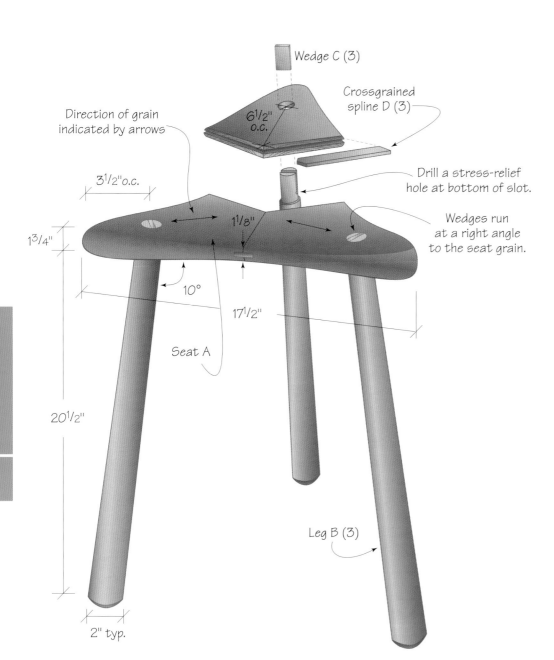

Wedge C (3)

Crossgrained
spline D (3)

Direction of grain
indicated by arrows

6$^{1}/_{2}$"
o.c.

3$^{1}/_{2}$"o.c.

Drill a stress-relief
hole at bottom of slot.

1$^{1}/_{8}$"

Wedges run
at a right angle
to the seat grain.

1$^{3}/_{4}$"

10°

17$^{1}/_{2}$"

Seat A

20$^{1}/_{2}$"

Leg B (3)

2" typ.

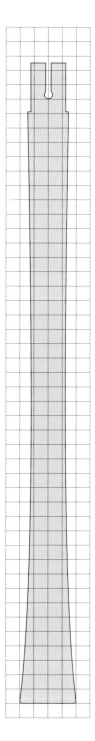

Each square
represents $^{1}/_{2}$".

INCHES (MILLIMETERS)

REFERENCE	QUANTITY	PART	STOCK	THICKNESS	(mm)	WIDTH	(mm)	LENGTH	(mm)
A	1	seat	walnut	$1^3/_4$	(45)	$15^1/_4$	(387)	18	(457)
B	3	legs	cherry	2	(51)	2	(51)	$22^1/_2$	(572)
C	3	wedges	poplar	$3/_8$	(10)	$1^1/_4$	(32)	$1^3/_4$	(45)
D	3	cross-grained splines	walnut	$1/_4$	(6)	1	(25)	6	(152)

Start with the Seat

To start the project, machine three $1^3/_4$" × 10" × 12" blanks for the seat. Next, make the joint cuts at 30° angles, as shown in step 1. Make the first cut and simply flip the blank for the second cut. Cut two of the blanks and place them together to start forming the seat. Make the two cuts on the remaining blank. Fit it to the other two blanks. If the three blanks don't fit together perfectly, adjust the fence on your table saw sled slightly and nibble on the third blank until the joints are perfect, or use a hand plane and fit the joints. Remember, removing just a slight amount of material will make all the difference between a so-so fit and a great fit.

Cut the grooves for the splines, as shown in step 2, then cut the splines for the grooves. The splines should smoothly fit into the grooves. If they are too snug now, after you apply the glue you will have great difficulty getting the splines to slide into the grooves. Also, the splines should fit snugly into the bottom of the grooves. You don't need to leave any glue space. Leave the splines long and trim them after the seat is assembled.

Bore a $1^1/_4$"-diameter hole in the blanks at a 10° angle toward the outside of the blanks, as shown in step 3. Hold the flat part of the blank against the fence. If the hole isn't aligned properly the legs will splay sideways.

Draw the shape of the scoop on one edge of the blanks. If you have a band saw with the capacity, rough-cut material from the blanks to form the cutout in the seat. You could also use a belt sander to do this job.

Dry assemble the seat blanks with the splines and draw the shape of the seat. Take the blanks apart and cut on these lines to create the outside shape of the seat, as shown step 4.

Double-check the fit of all the parts. You shouldn't have to apply any more clamp pressure than is needed to pull the parts together snugly. No amount of clamping pressure will make the joints fit any better if it doesn't go together now. If the joints don't fit properly, trim them until they do. Apply a thin coat of glue to the splines and slide them into the grooves. Coat the edges of the blanks and clamp it all together.

After the glue is dry, trim the splines flush to the edges of the seat. Then draw the seat scoop lines on the edges of the seat. Use your belt sander as a sculpting tool and shape the seat. Then use a random-orbit sander with 60-grit sandpaper to round all the edges of the seat. Work your way up to 220-grit sandpaper.

1 The joint cuts on the seat are at 30° angles. Make the first cut and simply flip the blank for the second cut.

2 When cutting the grooves for the splines, be sure to keep the splines in the lower half of the seat. You will be scooping out the top and you don't want to get into the splines.

3 This is one of those rare times when the fence needs to be parallel to the front of the drill press table. When boring your holes into the seat, this will keep the orientation of the hole square to the blank. (If the hole wasn't drilled at an angle, this wouldn't matter.)

Forming the cutout in the seat is easier to do now rather than after the seat blanks are glued together.

4 Create the outside shape of the seat, using your table saw.

Use your belt sander as a sculpting tool to shape the seat. This is not too difficult to do, but remember to use a light touch.

When gluing up the seat, don't use too much glue. You don't want any glue interfering with the seating of the splines in the bottom of the grooves.

Legs Last

Now it's time to turn the legs to shape. As you turn the tenons, check the fit as needed. The tenon should slip into the hole with a light twist. If it is too snug, you will have problems at glue-up time.

Step 5 shows a safe and simple way to cut the slots in the tenons. First, drill a $1\frac{1}{4}$"-diameter hole in a thick scrap of wood and use this as a fixture to hold the leg tightly as you cut the slot. Center the slot in the tenon. Now drill a $\frac{1}{4}$"-diameter hole along the base of the slot to ease the pressure on the leg when the wedge is inserted into the tenon. This hole will prevent the leg from splitting during assembly.

Cut the wedges from a wood that contrasts with the color of the legs. The wedges should be inserted into the slots about three-fourths of the depth of the slot when they are driven home. Once again, dry fit all the parts (don't drive the wedges in yet!). Apply a light coating of glue to the tenons and insert the legs. Put a generous coating of glue on the wedges and drive them home. Don't put any glue into the slots in the tenons because this glue will run to the bottom of the slot, the wedge won't seat properly and the hydraulic pressure will split the leg as the wedge is driven into place.

After the glue is dry, cut the wedges flush with the seat. Sand the tops of the legs smooth and level with the seat. Don't sand any more than necessary or you will sand the softer seat material lower than the tops of the legs.

I finished the stool with three coats of wipe-on polyurethane. Then I sat on the stool to plan my next project.

When turning the legs, check the width often to make sure it fits in the seat blank.

5 Here's how I cut the slots for my tenons.

When inserting the wedges into the seat, be sure to orient the wedges at a right angle to the wood grain of the seat.

Arts & Crafts Bookcase

BY KARA GEBHART

My mom has a bookcase in every room of my parents' house. Most of them are stuffed two rows deep with paperbacks, hardbacks, picture books and travel books. And still, whenever I visit, I find even more novels piled on top of end tables, underneath coffee tables, near the sides of chairs and on the backs of toilets. But I'm like her; I love collecting books.

Tired of moving my own piles of books every time I needed a place to set a drink down, I decided to build a bookcase of my own. This project serves as a nice challenge for the beginning woodworker and as a great weekend project for those more skilled. Its Arts & Crafts style is emphasized by mortise-and-tenon joinery, wedges and Stickley-style (sans ammonia) finish. While the ends remain forever assembled, a few good whacks to the wedges and the whole project comes apart, stacks together and can be transported easily in the trunk of a car.

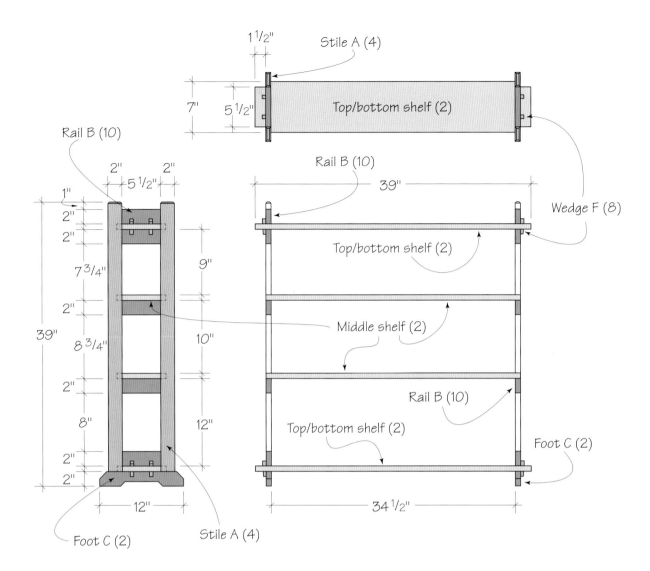

INCHES (MILLIMETERS)

REFERENCE	QUANTITY	PART	STOCK	THICKNESS	(mm)	WIDTH	(mm)	LENGTH	(mm)	COMMENTS
A	4	stiles	white oak	¾	(19)	2	(51)	38	(965)	1" (25mm) tenon, one end
B	10	rails	white oak	¾	(19)	2	(51)	7	(178)	¾" (19mm) tenon, both ends
C	2	feet	white oak	¾	(19)	2	(51)	12	(305)	
D	2	top & bottom shelves	white oak	¾	(19)	7	(178)	39	(991)	
E	2	middle shelves	white oak	¾	(19)	7	(178)	36	(914)	
F	8	wedges	white oak	½	(13)	½	(13)	2⅛	(54)	

hardware & supplies

4 oz. J.E. Moser's Golden Amber Maple water-based aniline dye, Woodworker's Supply

1 qt. Valspar Professional Glaze, warm brown/mahogany, WoodFinishingSupplies.com

Getting Started

In keeping with the Arts & Crafts tradition, I bought rough quarter-sawn white oak for this project, which I jointed and planed. Don't have a jointer or planer? No problem. Head out to your local home center and purchase dimensional lumber. The shelves can be cut from 1×8s, as can the rails and stiles, with some waste.

When purchasing your lumber, be picky. Choose knot-free heartwood (you don't want pieces with a lot of sap) that has lots of figure. Determine which pieces are the most attractive and mark those for the most visible parts of the project. Cut all your pieces to size according to the materials list.

Test Mortise

The first step to building this bookcase is tackling the joinery and assembling the sides. It's important that the project's tenons fit snugly into the mortises, which means first making a test mortise. This will allow you to check the size of your tenons throughout the tenon-cutting process, ensuring accuracy. This projects has 24 mortises. Do yourself a favor and, if you don't already have one, buy a hollow chisel mortising machine (about $250). A mortising attachment for your drill press or a $3/8$" Forstner bit also are acceptable options.

To make your test mortise, first select a piece of scrap from this project. Some sappy waste will do just fine. As a rule of thumb, mortises should be half the thickness of your tenon's stock. Because this project's tenon stock is $3/4$" thick, the mortises need to be $3/8$" thick. It's also a good idea to make your mortises about $1/16$" deeper than the tenons are long. This will keep the tenons from

bottoming out in the mortises. The depth isn't as important as the width in a test mortise, so simply make your test mortise as deep as your longest tenon is long. Because the rails B have $3/4$"-long tenons and the stiles A have 1"-long tenons, your test mortise for this project needs to be $1^{1}/_{16}$" deep.

If you've never used a hollow chisel mortiser before, check out "A New Manual for Mortisers" (*Popular Woodworking* magazine, August 2001 issue #123, available for sale online at www.popwood.com). Cut your test mortise.

Table-Saw Tenons

Now it's time to cut the 24 tenons. Sure, this sounds like a lot, but with a dado stack and a miter gauge, you'll breeze through this step in no time.

First, install a $5/8$" dado stack in your table saw. Set the fence for the finished length of your tenon and set the height of the dado stack to about $3/16$", which is the depth of your shoulders on your tenon. I cut the tenons on the rails B first, so the finished length was $3/4$". Hold the piece about $1/16$" from the fence and push it through the blade, using your miter gauge. Now, hold the piece directly against the fence and, using your miter gauge, push it through the blade again. Repeat this same procedure for the edges of the tenon.

After you've cut your first tenon, make sure that it fits snugly into your test mortise. If you're satisfied, keep cutting. Remember to set the fence for 1" once you're ready to cut the tenons on the end of the stiles A.

A few quick passes are all it takes to cut one side of the rails' tenons, using a dado stack and a miter gauge.

Use a test mortise to check the fit of your tenons throughout the tenon-cutting process. This ensures accuracy.

Back to the Mortiser

To cut the mortises, first use the drawings to measure where the rails B start and stop along the stiles A. Now, use your rails B to lay out the locations of your mortises (as shown at right). Cut each mortise a little over each measured line so that you're able to maneuver the rails for perfect positioning during glue-up. Cut all the mortises in the stiles A. You'll cut the mortises in the feet C after the sides of the bookcase are assembled.

Before assembling the sides, use your table saw, plane or chisel to cut a $^3/_{16}$" × $^3/_{16}$" chamfer on the top four edges of the stiles A, which is a traditional Arts & Crafts look.

Assembling the Sides

Now that the rails B and stiles A are complete, it's time to assemble the sides. First, dry fit everything together. Choose the face sides of your pieces carefully. Remember, your most visible pieces should be your most attractive. Clamp the assembly together.

Check for gaps, squareness, mistakes or anything else that might cause panic during gluing. Use the extra space you cut (when you mortised slightly over the measured lines) to maneuver the rails B until they're in their appropriate places. If it's tight, try hitting them with a mallet. Once you're positive that everything is perfectly positioned, use a ruler to draw lines across the joints. These lines will be your guides during glue-up. Now, take everything apart, put glue in the mortises, clamp and let dry.

Band-Sawn Feet

Once the glue has cured, it's time to cut the feet C. Each foot has two mortises and a detail cut using the band saw. Use the diagram to lay out the shape of the feet C on each piece. Lay out and cut your mortises, again going a little over each line for maneuverability during assembly.

Use the edges of the rails' tenons like rulers to mark the beginning and end of each mortise in the stiles.

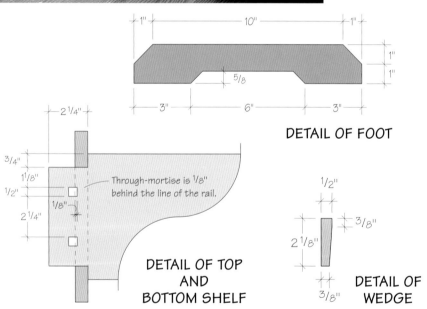

Slide an extra rail (which is $^3/_4$" thick) into the space between the top two rails to ensure a perfect slot for the top shelf.

DETAIL OF FOOT

DETAIL OF TOP AND BOTTOM SHELF

DETAIL OF WEDGE

Now, head over to your band saw. Cut the feet C to shape as close to your lines as you possibly can. The closer you get, the less cleanup you'll have to do. Remove the saw marks with a chisel or a plane. Dry fit the sides and feet, draw your guide lines, take the sides and feet apart, and then glue the assembly together.

Sturdy Shelves

With the sides now assembled, it's time to cut the shelves. First, you need to cut notches in the shelves' corners. The notches in the top and bottom shelves D are $2\frac{1}{4}$" long by $\frac{3}{4}$" wide, allowing enough overhang for the wedges. The notches in the two middles shelves E are $\frac{3}{4}$" long by $\frac{3}{4}$" wide.

Once you've measured and drawn where the notches start and stop, head to the table saw to cut the notches on the top and bottom shelves D. Because the table saw's blade is curved and because you won't be running the entire length of the board through the blade, you must be a little creative in your cutting. First, correctly position your fence and raise your blade to its appropriate height. Then, with a grease pencil, draw a line on the fence where the blade enters the table. Now, draw a line on your work where the cut should stop. Run the piece through until the two lines meet, then stop and pull the piece back. Carry the line on the piece over to the other side, flip the shelf over, and again run it through until the two lines meet, as shown in the top photo.

Head to your band saw and cut the remaining part of the top and bottom shelves' notches away. Now, cut the notches on the middle shelves, using the band saw.

The whole bookcase is held together tightly by tapered wedges F that snug into through-mortises in the top and bottom shelves D. Cut the mortises in the top and bottom shelves D, as shown at right.

Use the drawings to measure where the stiles start and stop on the feet. Like the rails, use the edge of the stiles' tenons like rulers to mark the beginning and end of each mortise.

When cutting the shelves' notches, draw a line on your table saw's fence to determine when to stop cutting. Because of the table saw's curved blade, more material will be cut away on the underside of the piece than on the top.

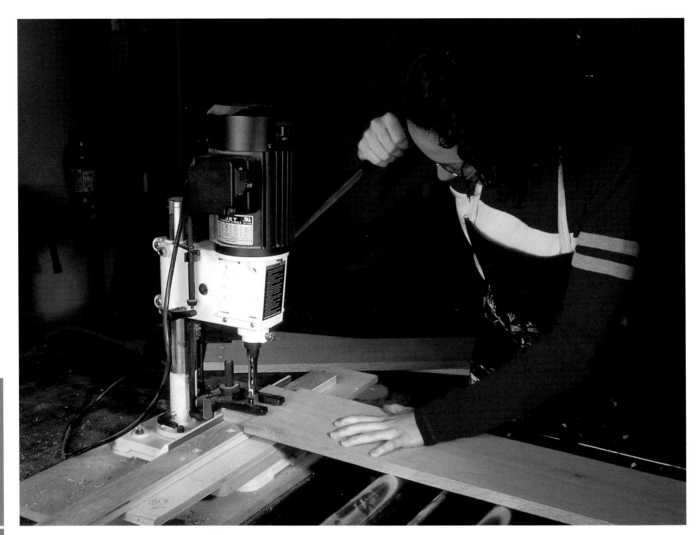

Wedges slide through mortised holes in both the top and bottom shelves. Use the drawings to lay out the locations of the $1/2$" x $1/2$" mortises. Note on the drawing how the mortises are located $1/8$" behind the line of the rails.

Tapered Wedges

If you haven't done so already, plane the stock for your wedges F down to ½" thick. Measure and make a mark ⅜" from the top of each wedge F, and another mark ⅜" wide from the bottom of each wedge. Draw a line, connecting your marks. Cut the taper, using either your band saw or a sander. Clean up the wedges with your chisel. Test fit the wedges F, as shown in the photo at right.

Finishing Touches

After all your hard work, the last thing you want to do is slack off when it comes to sanding. First, clean up all your edges with a sanding block and a chisel. Next, sand everything, starting with 100 grit and moving on to 150. Hold each piece up to a light, making sure you have all the scratch marks removed. Don't forget to break the edges.

Because this is an Arts & Crafts piece, I decided on a Stickley-style finish, without ammonia's danger. First, apply J.E. Moser's Golden Amber Maple water-based aniline dye. Let it dry overnight. Next, apply Valspar Professional warm-brown glaze. Let it, too, dry overnight. Finally, apply your favorite top coat. Check out the supplies list at the back of the book for ordering information. For complete instructions on how to create this ammonia-fumed-looking hue, see "Arts & Crafts Finish" (*Popular Woodworking* magazine, June 2002 issue #128, available for sale online at www.popwood.com).

Most of the tapered part of the wedges should slide through each mortise. As the wedge gets wider, you will need a mallet and a block of wood to finish pounding them down to a uniform height.

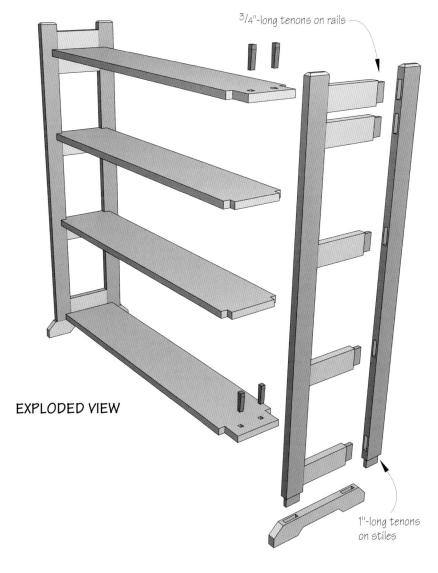

3/4"-long tenons on rails

EXPLODED VIEW

1"-long tenons on stiles

Shaker Firewood Box

BY DAVID THIEL

If you haven't already stumbled on the concept of storing a larger cache of logs indoors, this Shaker reproduction will provide a stylish location for your wood stash. Using pine, this project is simple enough to complete in a weekend.

First, cut all your pieces to length. Plane them down to $\frac{3}{4}$" thickness. You'll almost certainly end up having to glue up some boards to attain the $20\frac{3}{4}$" width. We opted to use biscuits to align the boards during the glue-up process.

Once the glue is dry, move to the next step — sizing the boards according to the materials list. Because you're working with a fairly plain wood and design, the attention you give to grain figure and to matching wood color will make the box more dramatic.

The next step is to lay out and cut the radius on the top front corner of each side A. Use the profile view on the next page to locate the beginning and ending points of the radius. Use trammel points set at a $10\frac{1}{2}$" radius to mark the corner, then use a jigsaw to cut both sides. Cut to the outside of the mark, allowing about $\frac{1}{16}$" overage to be sanded off. You may want to clamp the two sides A together for a final sanding to make sure the two radii match.

The next step involves cutting rabbets. I used two processes for this step. For the $\frac{3}{4}$" × $\frac{1}{2}$" rabbets I used the table saw, first running the $\frac{3}{4}$" dimension with the piece flat to the table, then the $\frac{1}{2}$" dimension with the piece on edge. Make sure your waste falls away from the fence to avoid binding

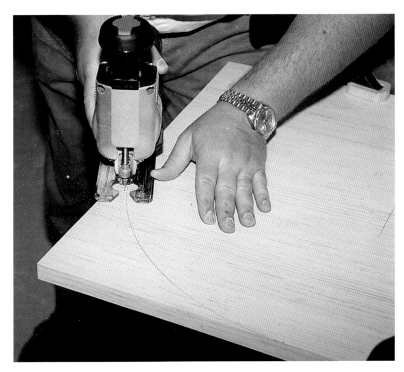

Use a jigsaw to cut the radius on the sides. Avoid tear-out by cutting from the inside of each piece.

The back panels are joined with $\frac{1}{4}$" x $\frac{1}{2}$" rabbets on opposing long edges. As I expected some wood shrinkage, I butted the pieces tightly together.

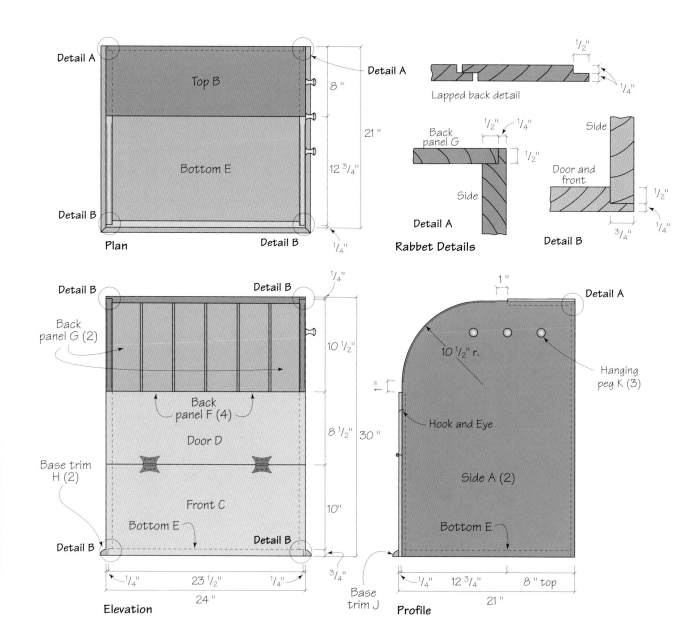

Plan

Detail A
Top B
Detail A
8"
21"
Bottom E
12 3/4"
Detail B
Detail B
1/4"

Rabbet Details

Lapped back detail
1/2"
1/4"

Detail A
Back panel G
1/2" 1/4"
1/2"
Side

Detail B
Side
Door and front
1/2"
3/4"
1/4"

Elevation

Detail B
Detail B
1/4"
Back panel G (2)
10 1/2"
Back panel F (4)
Door D
8 1/2" 30"
Base trim H (2)
Front C
10"
Bottom E
Detail B
Detail B
1/4" 23 1/2" 1/4"
24"
3/4"

Profile

1"
Detail A
10 1/2" r.
Hanging peg K (3)
1"
Hook and Eye
Side A (2)
Bottom E
Base trim J
1/4" 12 3/4" 8" top
21"

INCHES (MILLIMETERS)

REFERENCE	QUANTITY	PART	STOCK	THICKNESS	(mm)	WIDTH	(mm)	LENGTH	(mm)
A	2	sides	pine	3/4	(19)	20 3/4	(527)	29 3/4	(756)
B	1	top	pine	3/4	(19)	8	(203)	24	(610)
C	1	front	pine	3/4	(19)	10	(254)	24	(610)
D	1	door	pine	3/4	(19)	8 1/2	(216)	24	(610)
E	1	bottom	pine	3/4	(19)	20	(508)	23 1/2	(597)
F	4	back panels	pine	1/2	(13)	4 3/16	(106)	29 3/4	(756)
G	2	back panels	pine	1/2	(13)	3 7/16	(87)	29 3/4	(756)
H	2	base trim	pine	1/2	(13)	1	(25)	21 5/8	(549)
J	1	base trim	pine	1/2	(13)	1	(25)	24 1/4	(616)
K	3	hanging pegs		1/2	(13)	1 1/4	(32)		

hardware & supplies

2 5/8" x 2" (16mm x 51mm) black butterfly hinges, Woodworker's Supply, #110-708

No. 20 biscuits

1 1/4" (32mm) finish nails

between the fence and blade of the table saw.

After making all the necessary $\frac{3}{4}$" × $\frac{1}{2}$" rabbets, set up a router with a $\frac{1}{2}$" × $\frac{1}{2}$" rabbeting bit with a pilot bearing. Use this setup to run the necessary rabbets to accept the back panels.

If you've not already done so, run the six back panels F and G down to $\frac{1}{2}$" thick and cut them to the finished size. Then adjust the router setup to cut a $\frac{1}{2}$" × $\frac{1}{4}$" rabbet and run the opposite long edges of the back panels F and one long edge of the back panels G. These rabbets give a shiplapped detail to the back of the box and allow for seasonal changes in the boards.

The next setup for your router uses the rounded portion of a Roman ogee bit to cut a cove profile on the radiused side A edges (see photo at top right).

I used an $\frac{1}{8}$" roundover bit to soften the perimeter edges of the door D and front C (don't round over the mating edges), and the front and sides of the top B.

Before assembly, take the time to finish-sand the interior and sand any surfaces that will be difficult to sand after assembly. You will also want to sand off any glue or board-matching irregularities at this time.

Assemble the box using $1\frac{1}{4}$" finish nails. Start by attaching the bottom E between the two sides A, flushing up the front edges of all three pieces. Use the top B to help establish the spacing while nailing the sides A. Flush the top B to the rear edge. Nail it in place.

Now that you've established the box, nail the front C into place across the bottom edge, check for square and then nail up the sides A.

The next step is to nail the back in place. You'll need to pay particular attention to spacing the back panels F and G to maintain a uniform spacing on the shiplapped joints.

By using a portion of a Roman ogee bit, a delicate detail is added to the radiused edges of the sides. A cove bit with a guide bearing will work nicely, too.

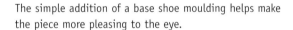

The simple addition of a base shoe moulding helps make the piece more pleasing to the eye.

Wrought-iron hinges add to the Shaker style of the piece and complete the reproduction look.

To add another detail to the box, I used a simple $\frac{3}{4}$" roundover bit to detail the top edge of the base trim pieces H and J. I then mitered the front corners and tacked the trim into place.

Now, mark the locations for the hanging pegs K. Next, drill your holes and then glue the pegs into place. Be aware of glue squeeze-out, or it will show when you put the finish on.

Now, sand the entire piece to get it ready for finishing. I opted for a simple coat of clear lacquer to show the natural beauty of the sugar pine while sealing and protecting the wood.

Once the finish has hardened it's time to put on the hardware. To keep with the traditional styling of the firewood box, I went with wrought-iron butterfly hinges. The hardware shown was found at a local specialty hardware store, but you can find similar pieces in the suppliers list at the back of the book. Attach the hinges to the door D. Then, attach the door to the front C.

Once the hardware's in place the only detail left is stocking the box with wood. When you're in from the cold, settle down for the evening in front of a cozy fire.

Boot Storage Bench

BY JIM STACK

This bench is more than just a place to sit down and take off your boots. You can also stow your skis and poles in the rack and slide your gloves onto the rabbit-ear dryers. There's plenty of room inside the bench to store extra hiking boots, work boots or maybe a pair of snowshoes. When the lid is closed, the continuous hinge provides plenty of strength for sitting.

I used sugar pine to build this bench, a wood I recommend. It's inexpensive and readily available in most areas. Plus, after texturing sugar pine, the wood looks like it was rescued from an old barn. Check out the end of this project to learn how to create a rough-sawn texture for your bench.

This bench is perfect for the beginner. Assembly is simple, requiring only biscuits and screws. Plus, you can complete this project in one long weekend.

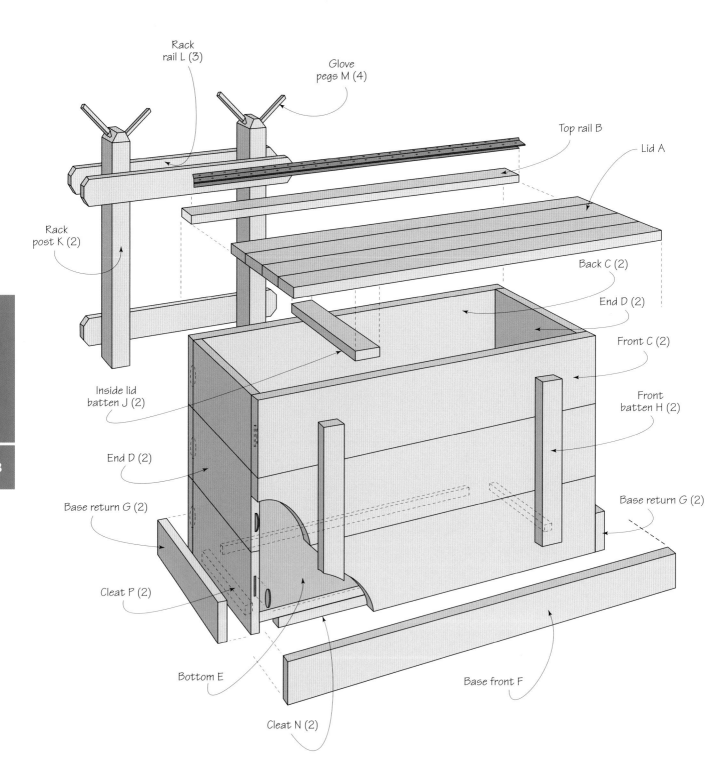

Rack
rail L (3)

Glove
pegs M (4)

Top rail B

Lid A

Rack
post K (2)

Back C (2)

End D (2)

Front C (2)

Inside lid
batten J (2)

Front
batten H (2)

End D (2)

Base return G (2)

Base return G (2)

Cleat P (2)

Bottom E

Base front F

Cleat N (2)

INCHES (MILLIMETERS)

REFERENCE	QUANTITY	PART	STOCK	THICKNESS	(mm)	WIDTH	(mm)	LENGTH	(mm)	COMMENTS
A	1	lid	sugar pine	1	(25)	13³⁄₈	(340)	35	(889)	
B	1	top rail	sugar pine	1	(25)	2	(51)	35	(889)	
C	2	front & back	sugar pine	³⁄₄	(19)	18	(457)	33	(838)	
D	2	ends	sugar pine	³⁄₄	(19)	18	(457)	12¹⁄₂	(318)	
E	1	bottom	sugar pine	³⁄₄	(19)	12¹⁄₂	(318)	31¹⁄₂	(800)	
F	1	base front	sugar pine	³⁄₄	(19)	3	(76)	34¹⁄₂	(876)	
G	2	base returns	sugar pine	³⁄₄	(19)	3	(76)	14¹⁄₂	(368)	
H	2	front battens	sugar pine	³⁄₄	(19)	2	(51)	12	(305)	
J	2	inside lid battens	sugar pine	³⁄₄	(19)	2	(51)	11	(279)	
K	2	rack posts	sugar pine	2¹⁄₂	(64)	2¹⁄₂	(64)	31	(787)	
L	3	rack rails	sugar pine	1	(25)	5	(127)	33	(838)	
M	4	glove pegs	sugar pine	1	(25)	1	(25)	7	(178)	³⁄₄" dia. x 1" (19mm x 25mm) tenon one end of peg
N	2	cleats	sugar pine	1	(25)	1	(25)	29	(737)	
P	2	cleats	sugar pine	1	(25)	1	(25)	12	(305)	

hardware & supplies

1 1¹⁄₂" x 35" (38mm x 889mm) continuous hinge

No. 20 biscuits

1¹⁄₂" wood screws

1 Cut out all the parts as shown in the materials list and glue up any panels you will need for the front and back C, ends D, lid A and bottom E. Using biscuits, glue the front and back C to the ends D first.

2 Check your box for squareness as you clamp by measuring the diagonals. The cauls on the corners help spread out the pressure exerted by the clamps, allowing you to use fewer clamps.

3 Install cleats N for attaching the bottom E about 1½" up from the bottom edge of the front and back C. Then screw cleats P onto the ends D in the same manner. These should be glued and screwed into place.

4 Drill oversize (¼") holes in the cleats N and P, drop the bottom E into place, and attach it with screws. These larger holes allow the screws to move with the solid-wood bottom, yet still hold it in place.

5 Now, glue the top rail B in place. The continuous hinge will be screwed to this rail and the lid A.

6 Cut the opposing bevels on the rack posts K, using the table saw with the blade beveled to 45° and a stop block attached to the miter gauge.

7 Simply roll the post K 180° to make the second cut.

8 Now, drill holes through the box ends D and front C, and attach the base front F and returns G with 1¼" wood screws and glue from the inside of the box.

9 Cut 45° bevels on the rack rails L, using the table saw or chop saw. Use two spacers, as shown in the photo, to keep the posts K parallel. Attach the rails L to the posts K with screws. Do not use any glue. Drill the ³/₄" holes for the glove pegs M. I used a Veritas ³/₄" power tenon cutter to cut the tenons on the ends of the pegs. This tenon cutter is available from Lee Valley Tools (item #05J41.02). If you don't own or don't want to buy a tenon cutter, ³/₄" dowels will work, too.

10 Drill oversize holes ($\frac{1}{4}$") in the back of the box where the posts K will be located, and screw the post assembly into place from the inside of the box, using four screws in each post K. Center the post assembly on the back of the box.

11 Screw the continuous hinge to the lid A first. Then stand the lid on the edge of the open hinge. Then drive the screws into the top rail B.

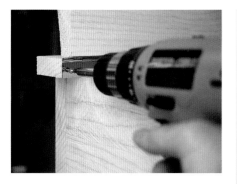

12 Attach the continuous hinge to the top rail B.

13 Attach battens H to the front with screws through oversize holes from the inside of the box. Now, attach the battens J to the lid A by screwing through holes in the battens into the lid. Now it's time to finish your bench. The great thing about giving wood a rough-sawn texture is that it can't be sanded. So put your sandpaper away. Brush or spray on a clear finish. Don't use a rag.

HOW TO CREATE A ROUGH-SAWN TEXTURE

Unplug the table saw and bend five or six teeth out of set by about $^{1}/_{16}$" (alternately bend the teeth; one to the right and the next to the left). Use a low-quality steel (not carbide-tipped) blade. The blade that came with your saw will probably do nicely.

The uneven saw-blade teeth provide rough-sawn results. Remember to wear eye protection.

After a pass through the saw, the boards look like they just came out of an old-fashioned circular sawmill.

Music Cabinet

BY CHRIS GLEASON

The day finally came when I decided to organize the bluegrass CDs and albums that had taken over virtually every horizontal surface in our living room. I searched local stores and the Internet and found a number of commercial CD racks on the market, but none that actually complemented our décor.

My wife and I knew what we wanted: Something refined but not too formal, and it had to store about 120 CDs and albums. While we like listening to our music, we don't get any particular pleasure from staring at rows of jewel cases while we entertain, so a door was a definite requirement.

The cabinet shown is our compromise. The CDs are stored in the upper section in nifty little spring-loaded CD racks that I ordered online. To eject a CD, just push it inward and it pops out into your hand. Albums are stored below, and I included a small cubby at the top for boxed sets, empty jewel cases and the rest of the stuff that tends to pile up around electronics equipment.

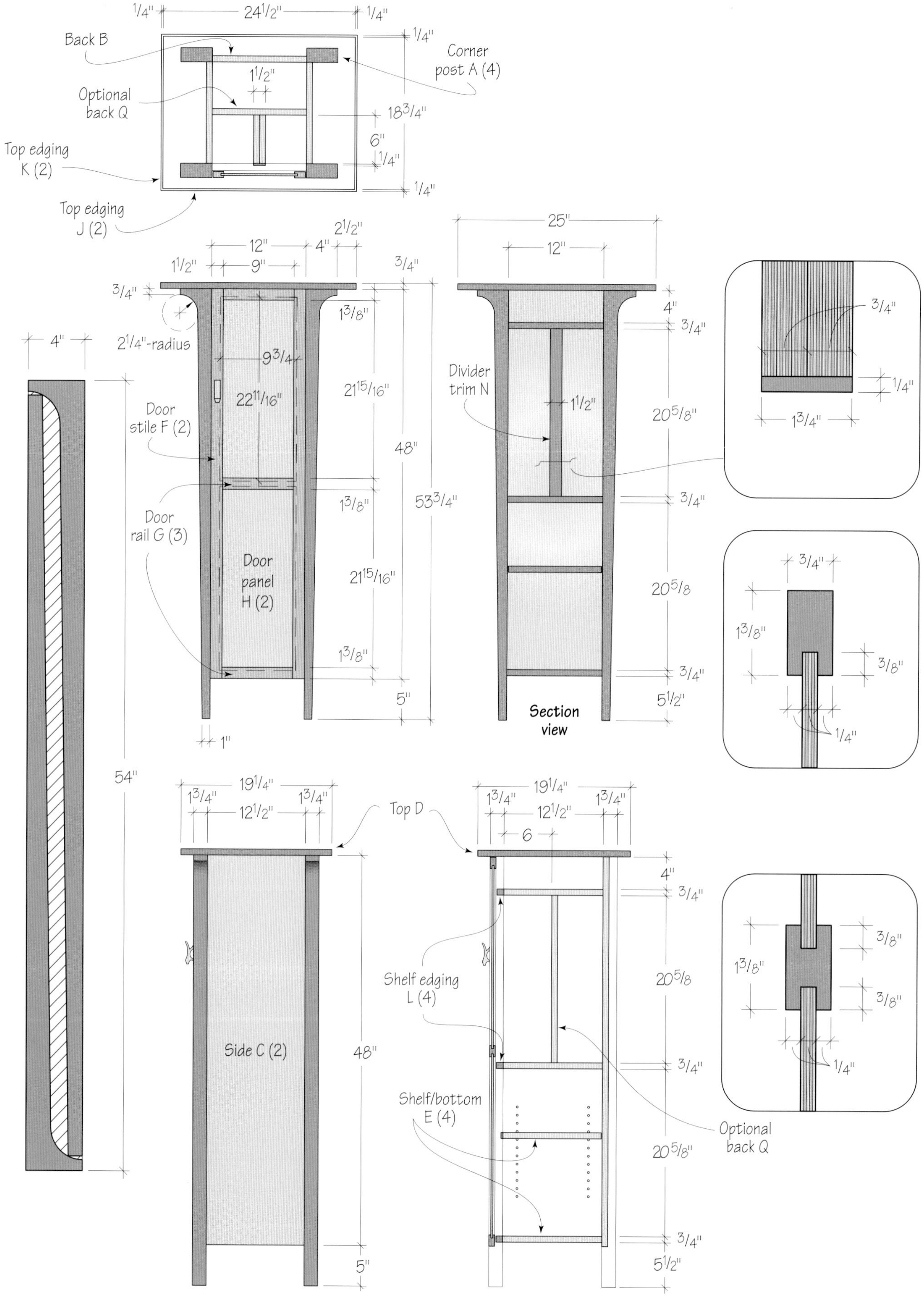

1/4"
24 1/2"
1/4"
Back B
1/4"
Corner post A (4)
1 1/2"
Optional back Q
18 3/4"
6"
1/4"
Top edging K (2)
1/4"
Top edging J (2)
25"
12"
4"
2 1/2"
1 1/2"
9"
3/4"
3/4"
2 1/4"-radius
1 3/8"
9 3/4
22 11/16"
21 15/16"
48"
Door stile F (2)
1 3/8"
53 3/4"
Door rail G (3)
Door panel H (2)
21 15/16"
1 3/8"
5"
1"
4"
54"
4"
3/4"
Divider trim N
1 1/2"
20 5/8"
3/4"
20 5/8
3/4"
5 1/2"
Section view
3/4"
1/4"
1 3/4"
3/4"
1 3/8"
3/8"
1/4"
19 1/4"
1 3/4"
1 3/4"
12 1/2"
Top D
19 1/4"
1 3/4"
1 3/4"
12 1/2"
6
4"
3/4"
Side C (2)
48"
5"
Shelf edging L (4)
20 5/8
3/4"
Shelf/bottom E (4)
20 5/8"
3/4"
5 1/2"
Optional back Q
3/8"
1 3/8"
3/8"
1/4"

INCHES (MILLIMETERS)

REFERENCE	QUANTITY	PART	STOCK	THICKNESS	(mm)	WIDTH	(mm)	LENGTH	(mm)	COMMENTS
A	4	corner posts	walnut	1¾	(45)	4	(102)	53	(1346)	nested pieces
A	1	back	birch plywood	¾	(19)	12	(305)	48	(1219)	
A	2	sides	birch plywood	¾	(19)	12½	(318)	48	(1219)	
A	1	top	birch plywood	¾	(19)	18¾*	(476)	24½*	(622)	
A	4	shelves & bottom	birch plywood	¾	(19)	12⅜*	(314)	12	(305)	
A	2	door stiles	walnut	¾	(19)	1⅜	(35)	48	(1219)	
A	3	door rails	walnut	¾	(19)	1½	(38)	9	(229)	
A	2	door panels	birch plywood	¼	(6)	9¾	(248)	22¹¹⁄₁₆	(576)	
A	2	top edging	walnut	¼	(6)	¾	(19)	25	(635)	
A	2	top edging	walnut	¼	(6)	¾	(19)	18¾**	(476)	
A	4	shelf edging	walnut	¼	(6)	¾	(19)	12	(305)	
A	2	vertical dividers	walnut	1½	(38)	6	(152)	20⅝	(524)	2 pieces of ¾"-thick plywood make up each divider
A	1	divider trim	walnut	¼	(6)	1½	(38)	20⅝	(524)	
A	1	door pull								
A	1	optional back	birch plywood	¾	(19)	12	(305)	20⅝	(524)	

*Sizes do not include ¼" edging

**Length reflects butt-joint edging, not mitered.

hardware & supplies

1 Amerock nonmortising hinge, Rockler #31495

1 Magnetic door catch, Rockler #30546

4 CD ejecting storage racks, Rockler #92908

  No. 20 biscuits

  No. 0 biscuits

  pocket-hole screws

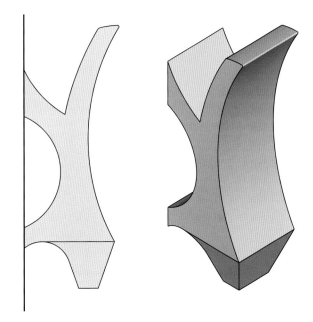

FULL-SCALE DOOR PULL PROFILE

Design and Construction

The cabinet is fairly simple in appearance, so I took the time to make a hand-carved door pull. I like the way this small detail contrasts with the larger swooping curves of the corner posts.

And because the door pull literally needs to be grabbed onto, it is a great opportunity to involve the viewer with the piece in a more thoughtful way. Inevitably, people who see the cabinet for the first time step back and admire the whole thing, then they lean in and carefully touch the handle to appreciate it up close.

My schedule doesn't allow a lot of time for me to work on furniture for my own home (we're all familiar with the shoemaker's barefoot children), so I needed to build the cabinet in a simple and relatively quick way. Using birch plywood allowed the case to come together quickly, and the solid walnut corner posts can be quickly band-sawn into a dramatic curved shape (essentially an oversize corbel, for those familiar with Arts & Crafts design elements).

Biscuits and pocket screws keep assembly simple, and the latter even help minimize the number of clamps you'll need for gluing up the case.

108

Mill the Corner Posts

Fabricating the corner posts A is straightforward. I like to try to get all four posts from a single board to ensure that they match in terms of color and figure, especially in a species like walnut that varies so much from one board to the next.

I established the overall dimensions of the piece by measuring the spot it was to occupy, then I made a full-size drawing to refine the proportions. I sketched some different shapes for the corner posts, incorporating different curves, tapers and flares. To make a template, I transferred the final shape to a $1/4$" piece of plywood. Transfer the pattern to some plywood, then carefully band-saw the shape and clean up the rough edges with a spindle sander or spokeshave.

Use the plywood template to transfer the pattern to 8/4 walnut boards,

After transferring my pattern to the corner post blanks, it's time to go to the band saw. A slow, steady feed rate provides a fairly smooth cut line. Remember to cut slightly wide of your mark, but keep it as tight as you can to reduce the amount of time you have to spend cleaning up the rough edges.

thicknessed to $1^{3}/_{4}$" and jointed on both edges. Trace the template with its flat (inside) edge against one jointed edge of the board, then flip the template over and nest a second post A on the same board. Use your band saw to cut the posts A to rough shape (cutting slightly wide of the line), then clean them up on the sander.

One way to keep the shapes uniform is to clamp or tape two pieces together and sand them both at the same time. It also lessens the time I spend sanding.

Prepare the Plywood Panels

Once the posts A are shaped, cut out the plywood panels for the cabinet parts. I typically rip the plywood into strips of the necessary widths and crosscut them on a table saw sled for accuracy, safety and speed. To avoid tear-out, feed slowly and use a sharp blade.

One drawback to using plywood is

the "exposed core" edges. Before assembling anything, I hide the exposed edges using $1/4$" edging strips J, K and L. The birch top D gets edged on all four sides, while the shelves and bottom E are edged only on the front. I used walnut edging to add contrast to the piece, gluing the edging on and holding it in place with painter's tape. In my opinion this is the least clamp-intensive (and easiest) method to attach edging, but if you've got the clamps, they're still a good idea.

I edged the sides of the top D, cut the edging flush with the front and back edges, and then edged the front and back edges. This leaves the buttjointed edging on the sides, making it less visible. You could also miter these joints for a more refined appearance. The shelves and bottom E are simply edged, then trimmed to length and planed flush.

The Side Assemblies

With the exception of a couple of holes, it's time to assemble the sides. While the sides C and back B are attached to the posts A using biscuits, I use pocket screws to attach the top D, bottom and shelves E. It's easier to drill the pocket holes in the sides C (to attach the top D) before assembling the sides, so on the inside face of the two sides C, drill two pocket holes at the top edge about 1" in from each edge. While you've got the drill out, you might as well drill the pockets in the shelves and bottom E, using the same spacing as on the sides C.

Assembling the cabinet is easiest when working in stages: You will first assemble the cabinet sides by sandwiching a plywood side C between two walnut corner posts A. Then glue the back B between the sides C. Finally, add the top D and shelves and bottom E.

I used biscuit joints to attach the plywood panels to the posts because it makes a strong, straightforward joint, and biscuits allow easy alignment of the parts.

All the panels align flush to the inside edge or corner of the posts A, making accurate biscuit alignment critical but still fairly simple. To mark the biscuit slot locations, I dry clamp the side assemblies first, holding everything tight and in place. On a joint of this length, I use about five biscuits, spaced a hand's width apart. The distance between the biscuits isn't critical, but make sure that your marks run evenly across the posts and the panel and that they're easily visible.

Unclamp the sides C, then clamp the rear posts A in place on either side of the back B, again holding the plywood flush to the inside of the posts. Mark locations for the back biscuits on the two edges (so they won't meet or interfere with the other slots), interspacing these slots between the slots for the side biscuits.

Remove the clamps and cut the slots for all the biscuits. By using the biscuit jointer with the fence set to cut in the center of a ¾"-thick panel, all the slots can be cut using the same setting by working from the inside surfaces.

After cutting the slots, it's not a bad idea to dry fit the parts with biscuits in the slots to make sure the slots went deep enough and are properly aligned.

Assembling the Cabinet

The first step is to glue the sides C between the posts A. When you're gluing up the sides, make sure you have a clean, damp paper towel on hand to immediately wipe away glue squeeze-out. The veneer used in plywood is usually very thin, so if you have to sand a lot to remove excess glue, you run the risk of burning through the veneer. Just like my old high school wrestling coach used to tell me, the best way to get out of a half nelson hold is to not get into one to begin with.

When the side assemblies are dry and sanded flush on the inside edges, it's time for you to glue that back B between the two side assemblies.

While this is drying, attach the top D with pocket-hole screws through the holes previously cut in the sides C. Just center the top D to split the overhang evenly side to side and front to back. If you want to plug these pocket holes, now's the time. Otherwise leave them as is because they're hardly visible.

With the back glued and clamped, I can go ahead and attach the top, then the bottom and permanent shelves. This photo lets you see the pocket screw holes drilled in the shelves. Once you have the shelf in the right location, clamp it to hold it in place, then drive the screws home.

Next, attach the upper shelf E with pocket-hole screws. To get the shelf spacing accurate, I simply rip scrap plywood into two 4"-tall spacers and insert them between the top D and the upper shelf E.

The bottom E is next. Rather than hold the bottom flush to the height of the sides, I hold it up ½" from the bottom edge to make aligning the door easier.

To install the middle shelf E, you can either measure and mark to evenly space the two openings, or just make two more ¼" plywood spacers to make it even easier. The shelf dividing the lower section is left adjustable to meet your needs.

If you decide to use the optional back Q install it at this time. Drill pocket holes in the front of the back. Using pocket screws, secure the back to the sides. When you put your CD's into the rack, the screw holes won't show.

Building the Door

While this appears to be a fairly traditional frame-and-panel door, it is somewhat unconventional in the way it goes together. Using a plywood panel is common in doors like this, but I take advantage of the plywood's dimensional stability and glue it into the frame on all sides. This creates an extremely durable and rigid door. To add some alignment and strength at the corners and center rail, I add a No. 0 biscuit.

Start by milling the door stiles F and rails G to 1⅜" wide by ¾" thick. Cut the pieces to length (two 48" stiles and three 9" rails), then cut a ¼"-wide by ⅜"-deep groove, centered on the inside edge of all the pieces. For the stiles, you may want to stop the groove short of the top to hide the groove from view. The middle rail will need a groove milled on its other side, as well, because it gets a panel H recessed into it on both its top and bottom edges.

Make sure the plywood door panels H fit in the grooves snugly; a sloppy fit will undermine this method of assembly. Once the plywood panels are cut to size, the door can be dry fit, then glued up.

Finishing Touches

Although I could've bolted on any number of store-bought door pulls, I'm glad I took the time to design one that works for this particular cabinet; it's a small detail that goes a long way. I build lots of pulls like this for cabinet doors, drawer fronts and jewelry box lids, and I always start by milling 8 or 10 oversize blanks in my wood species of choice. This allows me to experiment with different shapes and refine as I go along. Sometimes I end up using the first one I cut, but I generally prefer the later ones in the series because as I work, I identify a particular design element (usually some sort of curve or

Gluing the plywood panels into the grooves in the door frames feels weird if you've ever done frame-and-panel doors with solid panels. You're not supposed to glue solid panels, but it's important here. You can see at the bottom of the photo that I let the groove run through on the stiles. It's not visible after assembly, but it does make adding the biscuit to the joint a little tricky.

other dramatic shape) that I play with until I feel like the pull really coordinates with the piece.

Once the door pull P has been attached with epoxy and/or a screw through the door stile, I varnish the entire cabinet inside and out.

Adding Storage

Installing the CD racks requires some methodical work because they're sold in left- and right-hand pairs. It took two pairs per space to adequately fill the height (the racks are 12¾" tall), and with four pairs in front of you, they could easily get mixed up. You'll also need to trim the bottom off half of them on the band saw or radial-arm saw to fit the space. You may have noticed that the CDs don't fill the cabinet from front to back. To allow enough space for my albums below, I ended up with some wasted space, though I'm sure you can think of something to store secretly behind your CD collection.

The racks are designed to screw to cabinet sides, so our cabinet needs a vertical divider M running up the center to mount the center racks. The divider is 1½" thick by 6" wide by 20⅝" long. It's made by gluing two ¾" pieces of plywood together, then adding a ¼"-thick walnut trim N to hide the plywood edge on the front.

I fasten the divider M into the cabinet with pocket-hole screws, drilling the pocket holes at the top and bottom of the center divider. The pocket-hole screws get covered by the CD racks, so there's no need to plug them.

Because you've now got a 6"-wide space to work in, screwing in the racks becomes a tight procedure. The best solution I've found was to borrow a friend's close-quarters right-angle drill, which convinced me to add one to my power tool wish list.

Hanging the Door

Mounting the door is the last step. I use a nonmortising, wraparound hinge because it doesn't require routing or chiseling out a mortise and because it offers a slight degree of adjustability by featuring elongated slots instead of just round holes.

First, I screw the top hinge to the back of the door. Then I place the door in its opening. I use a craft knife to mark the top and bottom positions of the hinge on the inside of the walnut corner post A and note how far in or out the hinge falls relative to the front edge of the post.

Open the door, eyeball the marks as well as both the fore and aft door positions, and screw in the hinge. If the door closes smoothly, put on the bottom hinge in the same manner. Any discrepancies in the position of the door can be adjusted by moving the screws up, down, left or right in the hinge's slots.

A simple magnetic catch on the top left corner of the door keeps things tight.

I consider this cabinet to be a good example of how a refined, durable piece can be constructed with relatively simple techniques. It is practical, elegant and gratifyingly straightforward. And I've finally got a fitting home for my ever-expanding collection of bluegrass music.

Installing the CD racks is tight work, so the close-quarters right-angle drill came in very handy. Too bad I had to borrow one, but a trip to the tool store will fix that shortly.

GUSTAV STICKLEY'S CRAFTSMAN FARMS
The Quest for an Arts and Crafts Utopia

Aldren A. Watson HAND TOOLS

Greene & Greene Side Table

BY STEVE SHANESY

If you don't mind a little cheating, you can make this table quite simply. You see, the "pegged" mortise-and-tenon joints aren't really pegged at all. They are simple dowel joints, and the "pegs" are merely inlaid and applied pieces of ebony. But if you feel even the slightest twinge of guilt about taking such short cuts — please don't worry. The brothers Greene & Greene, renowned architects and designers of the late Arts & Crafts period, didn't hesitate a moment to use screws in their classic furniture. So a little liberty on this project follows right along in the tradition.

I built this table from cherry. The legs require 2"-thick material, and the top requires $1\frac{1}{2}$"-thick stock. The aprons and stretchers finish out at $\frac{7}{8}$" thick. If you use thinner material, you could reduce both the top and legs by $\frac{1}{2}$", and the aprons and stretchers could go to $\frac{3}{4}$" stock. That will keep the proportions just about right.

Prepare all your stock to the final sizes as given in the materials list. Next, prepare the template for routing the so-called cloud lift patterns on the aprons and stretchers. These are a Greene & Greene signature design and were borrowed from the Japanese.

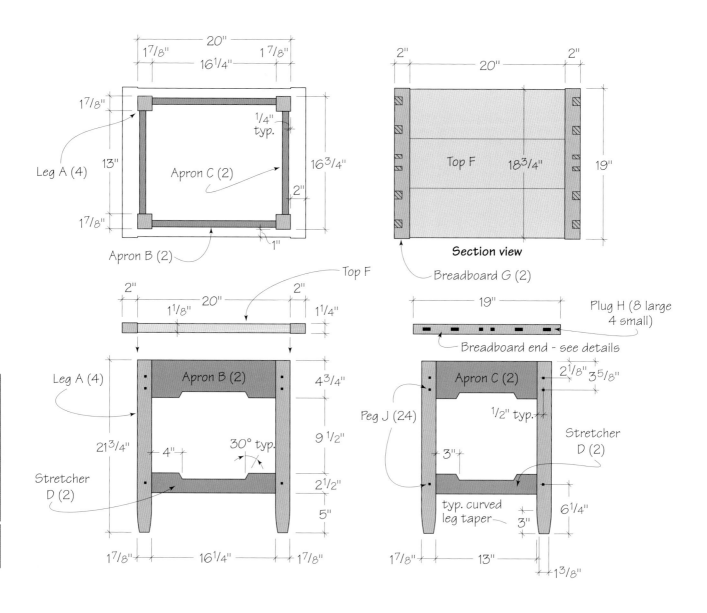

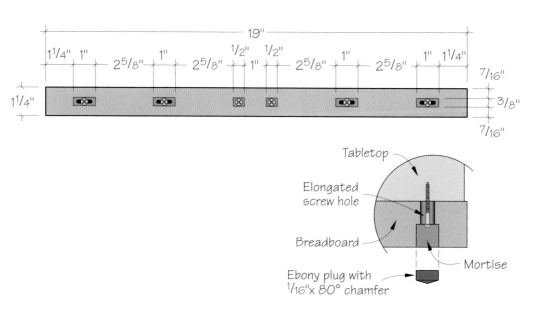

REFERENCE	QUANTITY	PART	STOCK	THICKNESS	(mm)	WIDTH	(mm)	LENGTH	(mm)	COMMENTS
A	4	legs	cherry	$1^7/_8$	(48)	$1^7/_8$	(48)	$21^3/_4$	(553)	
B	2	aprons	cherry	$^7/_8$	(22)	$4^3/_4$	(121)	$16^1/_4$	(413)	
C	2	aprons	cherry	$^7/_8$	(22)	$4^3/_4$	(121)	13	(330)	
D	2	stretchers	cherry	$^7/_8$	(22)	$2^1/_2$	(64)	$16^1/_4$	(413)	
E	2	stretchers	cherry	$^7/_8$	(22)	$2^1/_2$	(64)	13	(330)	
F	1	top	cherry	$1^1/_8$	(29)	$18^3/_4$	(476)	20	(508)	
G	2	breadboards	cherry	$1^1/_4$	(32)	2	(51)	19	(483)	
H		plugs	ebony	$^3/_8$	(10)	$^1/_2$	(13)	12	(305)	cut to length as needed
J		pegs	ebony	$^1/_4$	(6)	$^1/_4$	(6)	12	(305)	cut to length as needed

hardware & supplies

$2^1/_2$" (64mm) screws

$^3/_8$" x 2" (10mm x 50mm) gluing dowels

Cloud Lift Template

The two-sided template is made from $^1/_4$" Baltic birch plywood with the two patterns (one is slightly longer than the other) cut on the long edges of the same piece. Plan on using the template along with a straight router bit with a bearing of the same dimension as the bit diameter. Draw the design on the plywood following the dimensions in the diagram. The "lift" is $^3/_4$". Before band-sawing to the line, drill $^1/_2$" holes in the inside corners of the pattern. Drilling these holes is much easier than band-sawing such a tight radius. After carefully band-sawing to the line, sand the band-sawn edges so that they are smooth and straight. Next, on the template, mark each pattern edge with a line that represents the ends of the two different lengths of aprons and stretchers used in the project.

Before using the templates to rout the design, first band-saw away most of the waste on the parts. Using the template, draw a pencil line of the design on each apron B and C or stretcher D and E, then band-saw to about $^1/_{16}$" from the line. The router will clean up the rest.

To prepare for routing, set up a router table with a router and the $^1/_2$" straight bit as mentioned earlier. No fence is required for this type of pat-

tern cutting. To begin routing, align the part so that the ends match up with the lines previously drawn and so that the leading edge of the pattern aligns with the edge of the part. Attach the part to the template using two small brad nails. You can putty the nail holes later, but even so, select the "b" side of the part that will go to the inside of the table base as the side to nail to. Run each part this way. If you use cherry, do your best not to hesitate in the corners of the cut to minimize burning.

When routing the cloud lifts, the top-mounted bearing on the straight router bit follows and duplicates the pattern shape onto the table apron. Before routing, most of the waste material is removed with a band saw. Note, the aprons ends are aligned with pencil marks on the template, and the part is held to the template with brad nails.

Here I'm rounding over the edges with a $^1/_4$"-radius router bit. Almost every edge on the project gets this treatment. The exception is where parts join together, such as the apron and stretcher ends, and apron top edge.

ADVANCED

115

Shape the Legs

Next, turn to the legs A. First, shape the bottom of each leg A to the gradual tapering curve as seen in the diagram. Start the detail 3" up from the bottom. The slight curved taper removes only $\frac{1}{4}$" per side at the end of the leg. Now, make a template of the pattern so you can draw a pencil line for each side of the leg. Then band-saw and sand to the line.

With the parts of the table base shaped, go back to the router table and insert a $\frac{1}{4}$" roundover bit in the router. Run the profile on all the long edges of the legs A, stretchers D and E and aprons B and C, except for the top edge of each apron, which remains square.

Dowel Joints for Base

To assemble the legs A, aprons B and C and stretchers D and E, drill the holes for the $\frac{3}{8}$" dowels and sand the parts to 150 grit. Use two 2"-long dowels for each joint and position them so that when assembled, the apron sets back $\frac{1}{4}$" from the outside face of the leg.

When all the dowel holes are drilled, dry fit the assembly before actually gluing it together. When I assembled my base, I glued and clamped it in two stages. First, assemble one set of legs, aprons and stretchers. Then complete the assembly after the first assembly is dry. Take care not to apply too much glue, because squeeze-out in the joint is difficult to clean up and can lead to finishing problems later.

Make the Top

Now, turn your attention to the top F. The breadboard ends with ebony plugs are another Greene & Greene signature detail. I made the breadboard ends G $\frac{1}{8}$" thicker than the top F, leaving them $\frac{1}{16}$" proud of the thickness of the rest of the top. They also are slightly longer. This additional length anticipates eventual expansion of the top.

Prepare your top's main boards and glue them up. When dry, square up the top F and cut it to its final size. The breadboards G are attached easily with a 2½"-long screw in each of the plugged holes.

Be sure to make elongated screw

116

Simple joinery makes this project quite easy. A pair of dowels join each apron and stretcher end to the leg. This vintage Stanley #59 doweling jig makes this process especially easy due to its adjustability (see the sidebar "Old Stanley Doweling Jig The Best"), particularly when drilling the holes in the legs to provide the $\frac{1}{4}$" setback of the aprons.

RIGHT-SIZING DOWELS

A dowel that's even slightly oversize in diameter can cause all sorts of problems — the worst of which is actually splitting the part to be doweled. This not only happens because the dowel is a snug fit, but also because the glue in the hole has nowhere to go once you insert the dowel. If the glue can't escape, it can prevent the dowel from inserting completely and can actually prevent the parts to be joined from closing completely.

If your dowels are too snug, there's an easy fix called a dowel skinner. In this project, I found my $\frac{3}{8}$" dowels were too tight for my $\frac{3}{8}$" hole. The solution was to drill in $\frac{1}{8}$"

or thicker mild steel a hole, that's $\frac{1}{64}$" smaller than the dowel. Then just drive your dowels through the hole with a hammer and you'll get a perfect fit.

OLD STANLEY DOWELING JIG THE BEST

There was a time when I used a lot of dowels in furniture building. Back then, the jig I used was the self-centering kind. A few years ago a woodworker friend showed me a vintage Stanley doweling jig he picked up at a flea market. Its design is quite similar to the current Stanley offering, but the quality of the materials is far superior to today's models.

The great feature of this design is the variability of spacing the dowel hole locations and the ease of aligning the

hole center to your predetermined location. Since purchasing my own vintage Stanley, my self-centering jig hasn't come out of the drawer. Chances are you can buy your own vintage Stanley #59 or #60 at auction on eBay (www.ebay.com). Just make sure the one you bid on is complete. The bushings for guiding your drill are interchangeable, depending on which size hole you want. A complete jig would include bushings for $1/4$", $5/16$", $3/8$", $9/16$" and $1/2$" drill bits. These rigs can generally be bought on eBay for about $25.

If you do buy one of these tools without bushings (or if you need odd-size bushings), Stanley still sells them as replacement parts. (See the suppliers list at the back of the book.)

No mortising machine? You can still speed along the process of cutting the plug holes in the breadboard ends. After marking out the locations, drill out most of the waste, then square up the ends and side walls with a chisel.

slots in the breadboard to anticipate wood movement in the top F. To make the square grooves in the breadboard ends, use a mortising machine or chain drill the holes and then square them up with a chisel. The depth of the hole is 1". The size of the small holes is $3/8$" wide by $1/2$" long. The longer holes are 1" long.

Before attaching the breadboards G to the top F, go back to the router table and round over the long edges of the top and the outside edges of the breadboards. The edges of the top and breadboards that join together remain square. As with the table base, presand the top before assembling the top and breadboard ends. When done, clamp the ends to the top so they remain in perfect position while screwing the ends in place.

Ebony Plugs and Pegs

The ebony plugs J used on the table all stand about $1/8$" proud of the surface.

The top of each plug is shaped so that it looks faceted, or slightly beveled on the top. The ebony plugs for the breadboards are first made as a $3/8$" by $1/2$" by 12"-long stick. Carefully make two 10° cuts on one of the long $3/8$"-dimension edges to create two of the facets. Next, cut them to length, but a little long. Fit each one as they are installed. I fit mine by sanding. Also sand the other two facets on the top surface. When ready to install, add a slight amount of glue and carefully tap them into place. The process is a bit tedious, but it takes just about an hour to complete.

The smaller pegs K for the mortise-and-tenon joints are $1/4$" square. To make these, cut an ebony stick $1/4$" square and about 12" long. Facet the top to make a shallow pyramid shape by sanding, then hand saw off the shaped end about $1/8$" long. Repeat the process until you have at least 24 pegs.

To apply the pegs, use cyanoacrylate glue. Carefully mark the location of each peg, add a tiny drop of glue, and set it in place. The glue cures quickly and no clamping is required.

Finish-sand the top and base with 220-grit sandpaper. This last sanding must be done by hand due to the plugs and pegs projecting off the surface. I finished the project using two coats of a clear satin finish spray lacquer that comes in an aerosol can. A wiping varnish or polyurethane also would be appropriate. Whichever finish you use, sand lightly between coats for the smoothest results.

You're almost done. Attach the top F to the base using whatever method you prefer. I used 1"-square wooden cleats and screws. Again, be sure your method of attachment accommodates wood movement in the top.

24-Hour Workbench

BY CHRISTOPHER SCHWARZ & KARA GEBHART

Whenever we leave beginning woodworkers to work alone in the shop, it's a fair bet that when we return to check on them, they're working on the shop's floor.

We have at least five workbenches in our shop — not counting the assembly tables — but the new people always seem to prefer the wide expanse of the concrete floor more than the benches. Of course, I shouldn't talk. When I started woodworking I had my grandfather's fully outfitted bench. But my first few projects were built on the floor of our back porch, my assemblies propped up on a couple of 4×4s. I can't for the life of me remember why I chose the floor instead of the bench.

Since those early years, I've built a few workbenches. And I've been striving to make each one more versatile, solid, inexpensive and quick to build than the last. I think I've finally got it. To test my theory, Kara Gebhart and I built this bench with a $180 budget and just 24 hours of working time in the shop.

That $180 includes the wood, the vise and the hardware. And that 24 hours includes everything, too, even the two hours we spent picking out the wood and sawing it to rough length on a dolly in the parking lot of the home-improvement center. (But once again, I was working on the ground. Oh, drat.)

The real beauty of this bench (besides getting you off the floor) is that it can be completed using tools you likely already have in your shop.

For this project, your must-have tools are a table saw, a drill press, a corded drill and some basic hand tools. If you have a jointer and planer, the project will go faster because you can easily dress your lumber to size and eliminate any bowing or warping. But don't be afraid to work with the lumber as it comes from the lumberyard. Just make sure you buy the straightest pieces you can.

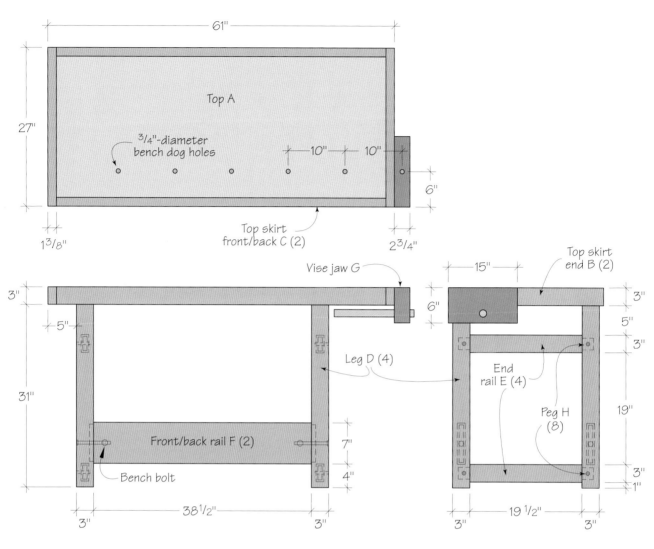

61"

27"

Top A

3/4"-diameter
bench dog holes

10"   10"

6"

Top skirt
front/back C (2)

1 3/8"

2 3/4"

3"

Vise jaw G

Top skirt
end B (2)

15"

3"

6"

5"

5"

3"

31"

Leg D (4)

End
rail E (4)

19"

Front/back rail F (2)

7"

Peg H
(8)

3"

Bench bolt

4"

1"

3"

38 1/2"

3"

3"

19 1/2"

3"

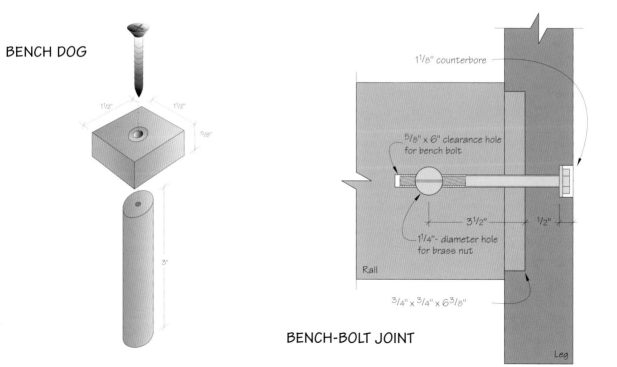

BENCH DOG

1 1/2"   1 1/2"

5/8"

3"

1 1/8" counterbore

5/8" x 6" clearance hole
for bench bolt

3 1/2"

1/2"

1 1/4"- diameter hole
for brass nut

Rail

3/4" x 3/4" x 6 3/8"

BENCH-BOLT JOINT

Leg

INCHES (MILLIMETERS)

REFERENCE	QUANTITY	PART	STOCK	THICKNESS	(mm)	WIDTH	(mm)	LENGTH	(mm)	COMMENTS
A	1	top	see comments	3	(76)	24¼	(616)	58¼	(1480)	top is laminated using four layers of ¾"-thick Baltic birch plywood
B	2	top skirt ends	yellow pine	1⅜	(35)	3	(76)	27	(686)	
C	2	top skirt front & back	yellow pine	1⅜	(35)	3	(76)	61	(1549)	
D	4	legs	yellow pine	3	(76)	3	(76)	31	(787)	
E	4	end rails	yellow pine	1⅜	(35)	3	(76)	23½	(597)	
F	2	front & back rails	yellow pine	1⅜	(35)	7	(178)	40	(1016)	2" (51mm) tenon, both ends
G	1	vise jaw	yellow pine	2¾	(70)	6	(152)	15	(381)	¾" (19mm) tenon, both ends
H		pegs	hardwood	⅜ dia.	(10)			2⅛	(54)	
J		benchdog dowels	hardwood	¾ dia.	(19)			3	(76)	make 2 - 4 dogs
K		benchdog piece	hardwood	⅝	(16)	1½	(38)	1½	(38)	

hardware & supplies

2½" (64mm) screws

4 5" (129mm) corner braces

1 set of four Veritas special bench bolts, Lee Valley Tools #05G07.01

1 large front vise, Lee Valley Tools #70G08.02

1 vise handle, Lee Valley Tools #05G12.03 No. 8 x 1¼" (32mm) screws

lumber

2½" (64mm) screws

3 2" x 8" x12' boards, preferably southern yellow pine (if available in your area) or vertical-grade fir

2 sheets of ¾" Baltic birch, Finnish birch or Appleby. This material comes in 60" x 60" sheets. Have the lumberyard rip them down the middle so you end up with four sheets of ¾" x 30" x 60".

Start with the Rough Stuff

Time: 0:00 to 5:06

In a nutshell, here's how the bench goes together: The top is made of four pieces of Baltic birch plywood that are laminated together with a pine skirt glued around the edge. On the bench's pine base, the end rails are joined to the legs using pegged mortise-and-tenon joints. The end assemblies attach to the front and back rails using an unglued mortise-and-tenon joint with big bench bolts; it's quite similar to a bed in construction.

When we first went to the lumberyard, it seemed like a good idea to buy 4×4 posts for the legs D. But when we got there (and later called around to other nearby lumberyards) we discovered that the only 4×4s available in yellow pine were #2 common, which has more knots than the #1 pine (also sold as "prime" or "top choice" in some yards). If you can't get yellow pine where you live, you can look for fir. (To find yellow pine in your area, visit www.southernpine.com.)

After picking through the mound of knotty 4×4s, we decided to instead make the legs D by ripping a 2×8 and gluing up the legs to the thickness that we needed. It took longer to make the legs this way, but now they have almost no knots.

Crosscut and rip the parts you need for the base of the bench and the skirt B and C that goes around the top A. If you have a planer and jointer, dress your lumber. Now, glue up and clamp the parts for the legs D and get out your clamp collection and some buckets (yes, buckets) to glue up the top A.

Top-Down Construction

Time: 5:06 to 6:29

I've built a few of these benches and have come up with a pretty easy way to make the top A: Just sandwich all the plywood into a nearly 3"-thick slab. We glued it up one layer at a time to keep things under control and to ensure we could eliminate all the gaps on the edges.

You're probably going to need at least four 8-ounce bottles of yellow glue for this part of the project, plus a scrap of plywood ($^1/_4$" × 4" × 7" worked for us) to spread the glue evenly. Squirt a sizable amount onto one piece of plywood and spread the adhesive until you've got a thin and even film. Place the plywood's mating piece on top and line up the edges. Now, drive about a dozen No. 8 × 1$^1/_4$" screws into the two pieces. Space the screws evenly across the face of the board, but you don't need to get scientific about it. The object is to pull the two pieces together without gaps. After 30 minutes of drying time, remove the screws and add another layer of glue, plywood and some more screws.

Because you don't want a bunch of screw holes staring at you every time you use the bench, you'll likely want to attach the final layer with clamps, clamping cauls and anything else heavy you have in your shop.

We used four cauls (a clamping aid) across the width of the top to put even more pressure in the middle. The cauls should be about 2" × 2" × 32". Plane or sand a $^1/_{16}$" taper toward each end to give each caul a slight bow. When you clamp the bow against the top, this will put pressure in the middle of your slab.

Finally, use whatever other clamps you have to clamp the edges (C-clamps work well).

When all four layers are glued together, cut your top A to its finished size using a circular saw and a straight scrap of wood to guide it. Because the top is so thick, you'll have to cut from both faces, so lay out cutting lines with care.

Use whatever clamps are on hand to glue the top together. If you're low on clamps, you can use 5-gallon buckets of water (they are quite heavy) in the middle, four cauls and C-clamps along the edges.

Skirt Will Test Your Skills

Time: 6:29 to 11:49

Now, gather the skirt pieces B and C and begin laying out the finger joints for the corners. These joints are mostly decorative. Butt joints or miters will do just as well (and save you some time). And if you want to make this process even easier, use $^1/_2$"-thick material for the skirt, which is a whole lot easier to clamp in place because it is more flexible than some of the thicker material.

Here's how we suggest you cut the finger joints: First, lay out the joints on the end pieces B with just one tongue or finger sticking out. Each finger is 1$^3/_8$" long and 1" wide. Cut the waste away using a handsaw or band saw and check the fit against your top A. When it fits perfectly, use these joints to lay out the mating joints on the long skirt pieces C. Cut the notches on the long skirt pieces C and check the fit of your joints. Tune them up using a chisel, a rabbet plane or a shoulder plane.

Now, glue the skirt pieces B and C to the top A. Because each ply in plywood runs the opposite direction of the ply above it, there's actually a fair amount of long grain on the edges of your top A. This means the skirt will stay stuck just fine using only glue. Add as many clamps as you can. While that glue dries, read the directions for installing the vise, because that's the next step.

The instructions that come with the Veritas vise are complete and easy to follow; it just takes some time to get everything moving smoothly. Before you begin, be sure your drill press's table is square to the chuck; this will save you lots of frustration. Once you get your vise installed, place the top A on a couple of sawhorses (you'll need a friend's help) and get ready to build the base.

A Stout Base

Time: 11:49 to 14:54

The base of this bench is built with mortise-and-tenon joints. The two assembled ends are glued together and then pegged using dowels. The ends are attached to the front and back rails using an unglued mortise-and-tenon joint plus bench bolts.

The first step is to make a practice mortise in a piece of scrap that you can use to size all your tenons. We made our mortises on a drill press using a $3/4$"-diameter Forstner bit and a fence. You can make really clean mortises this way. After you've made your test mortise, head to the table saw to make all your tenons.

I make my tenons using a dado stack in my table saw. The fence determines the length of the tenon; the height of the dado blades determines the measurement of the tenons' shoulders. Set the height of the dado stack to $5/16$", cut a tenon on some scrap as shown in the photos, and see if it fits your test mortise. If the fit is firm and smooth, cut all the tenons on the front and back rails F and end rails E.

Now, use your tenons to lay out the locations of your mortises on the legs D. Use the diagrams as a guide. Cut mortises using your drill press and get ready to install the bench bolts.

The skirt pieces can be joined using finger joints, a miter or just wood screws. If you choose finger joints, your best bet is to lay out and cut the joint on one member and then use that joint to lay out your cut lines on its mate.

The easiest way to make clean mortises using your drill press is to first drill a series of overlapping holes. Then go back and clean up the waste between these holes several times until the bit can slide left to right in the mortise without stopping. Then you only have to square up the ends with a chisel.

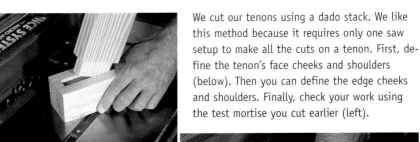

We cut our tenons using a dado stack. We like this method because it requires only one saw setup to make all the cuts on a tenon. First, define the tenon's face cheeks and shoulders (below). Then you can define the edge cheeks and shoulders. Finally, check your work using the test mortise you cut earlier (left).

Big Bad Bench Bolts

Time: 14:54 to 18:59

The set of bench bolts for this project set us back $20, but they are worth it. There are less expensive alternatives to this specialty hardware, but none are as easy to put together.

You can begin installing the bench bolts by drilling in the legs D a 1⅛"-diameter by ½"-deep counterbore that's centered on the location of the rail F. Then drill in the center of that counterbore a ⅝"-diameter hole that goes all the way through the leg into the mortise you cut earlier.

Now, dry assemble the ends plus the front and back rails F and clamp everything together. Use a ⅝" brad-point drill bit to mark the center of your hole on the end of each tenon.

Disassemble the bench and clamp the front rail F to your top A or in a vise. Use a doweling jig and a ⅝" drill bit to continue boring the hole for the bench bolt. You'll need to drill about 3¾" into the rail. Then repeat this process on the other tenons.

Now, you need to drill a 1¼"-diameter hole that intersects the ⅝" hole you just drilled in the rail.

This 1¼"-diameter hole holds a special round nut that pulls everything together. To accurately locate where this 1¼" hole should be, I made a simple jig I picked up from another project. This works like a charm, and I recommend you use one. Sometimes drill bits can wander — even when guided by a doweling jig — and this simple jig ensures success.

Plane or sand all your legs and rails, then assemble the bench's base. First, glue the end rails E between the legs D. Glue and clamp that assembly. When it's dry, drill a ⅜"-diameter by 2"-deep hole through each joint. Then glue and hammer a peg H through the tenons using 2⅛"-long sections of ⅜"-diameter dowel stock into each hole. Then install the bench bolts and use a ratchet and socket to snug your bolts and bring everything together.

Now, screw the 5" braces J to the legs as shown on page 125. Turn the

Once you've drilled the counterbore and the through-hole for the bench bolt, mark its location on the end of the tenon using a brad-point bit.

top upside down on the sawhorses and place the assembled base in position. Screw it down.

Dog Holes and Details

Time: 18:59 to 23:02

Dog holes on a bench are essential for clamping large panels, holding table legs and even clamping difficult-to-clamp assemblies. Most round dog holes are ¾" in diameter so they accept a wide range of commercial dogs.

We made our own dogs for this bench to keep us from blowing our $180 budget. (If your budget isn't as strict, we recommend the Veritas brass Bench Pups, #05G04.04.

Our homemade dogs are made using 3"-long sections of ¾" dowel K screwed to ⅝" × 1½" × 1½" pieces L of scrap hardwood.

First, drill the dog hole in your tail vises jaw G using your drill press. While you have the vise jaw G off the bench, go ahead and add the edge detail of your choice to the ends. We chose a traditional large bead. A chamfer would be quicker if you're pressed for time.

Now, put the vise jaw G back on and lay out the locations of your dog holes in the top A. They can be anywhere from 8" to 11" apart. You'll have to build a simple jig to cut the holes. It's made from three pieces of scrap and is shown in action in the photo on the next page.

We bored the dog holes using a ¾" auger bit in a corded drill. Use a low

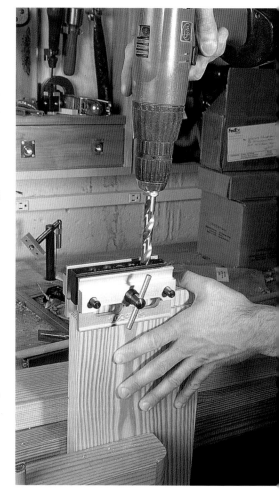

Drill a hole for the bench bolt using a doweling jig and a ⅝"-diameter drill bit. It's a deep hole, so you might need an extralong bit to do the job.

speed on your drill for this operation because you need buckets of torque.

Now, chamfer the rim of each dog hole; this prevents the grain from ripping up when you pull the occasionally stubborn dog from its hole (bad dog!). You can just use a chamfer bit in your plunge router to make this cut. Or you can simply ease the rims using some coarse sandpaper.

We sanded the top A by using 120-grit sandpaper in a random-orbit sander and called it a day. Break all the sharp edges using 120-grit sandpaper. You don't need a fancy finish on this bench — just something to protect it from spills and scrapes. We took some off-the-shelf satin polyurethane, thinned it down to three parts poly and one part mineral spirits, and ragged on two coats. Allow the finish to dry at least four hours between coats. (No, the four hours of drying time isn't included in our total time.)

Then we turned the stopwatch off and checked our time: 23 hours and 2 minutes. We had just enough time left to sweep the floor in case someone else needed to work down there.

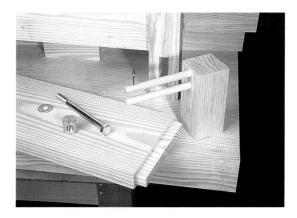

To accurately position the hole for the brass nut shown in the photo, build a simple jig like the one shown here using a $^5/_8$" dowel, a scrap of wood and a nail. The nail is located where you want the center of the brass nut to go. Insert the dowel into the hole in the rail and tap the nail. Then just drill a $1^1/_4$"-diameter hole there and your joint will go together with ease.

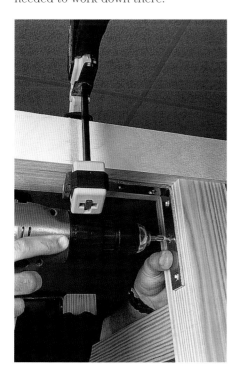

Installing the brackets that secure the top to the base is simple with this trick. Lay a scrap board across the legs and clamp the bracket to it. Now screw the bracket to the leg.

Here you can see our dog-hole drilling jig in action. There are two $^3/_4$" holes in the plywood base: one for the bit and the other to allow us to see the layout marks on the bench top.

suppliers

ADAMS & KENNEDY — THE WOOD SOURCE
6178 Mitch Owen Road
P.O. Box 700
Manotick, Ontario
Canada K4M 1A6
613-822-6800
www.wood-source.com
Wood supply

BALL AND BALL
463 West Lincoln Highway
Exton, Pennsylvania 19341
800-257-3711
www.ballandball-us.com
Antique hardware reproductions

B&Q
B&Q Head Office
Portswood House
1 Hampshire Corporate Park
Chandlers Ford, Eastleigh
Hampshire, U.K.
SO53 3YX
0870 0101 006
www.diy.com
Tools, paint, wood, electrical, garden

BRIMARC ASSOCIATES
7-9 Ladbroke Park
Millers Road
Warwick, U.K.
CV34 5AN
01926 493389
www.brimarc.com
Woodworking tools and accessories

CONSTANTINES WOOD CENTER
1040 East Oakland Park Boulevard
Fort Lauderdale, Florida 33334
800-443-9667
www.constantines.com
Tools, woods, veneers, hardware

CRAFT SUPPLIES USA — THE WOODTURNERS CATALOG
1287 East 1120 South
Provo, Utah 84606
800-551-8876
www.woodturnerscatalog.com
Master's Magic

FOCUS (DIY) LIMITED
Gawsworth House
Westmere Drive
Crewe
Cheshire, U.K.
CW1 6XB
0800 436 436
www.focusdiy.co.uk
Tools and home woodworking equipment

HOMEBASE LTD.
Beddington House
Railway Approach
Wallington
Surrey, U.K.
SM6 0HB
0845 077 8888
www.homebase.co.uk
Tools and home woodworking equipment

THE HOME DEPOT
2455 Paces Ferry Road
Atlanta, Georgia 30339
800-553-3199 (U.S.)
800-668-2266 (Canada)
www.homedepot.com
Tools, paint, wood, electrical, garden

HORTON BRASSES INC.
49 Nooks Hill Road
Cromwell, Connecticut 06416
800-754-9127
www.horton-brasses.com
Reproduction cabinet and furniture hardware

HOUSE OF TOOLS
100 Mayfield Common Northwest
Edmonton, Alberta
Canada T5P 4B3
800-661-3987
www.houseoftools.com
Woodworking tools and hardware

LANGEVIN & FOREST
9995 Boulevard Pie IX
Montreal, Quebec
Canada H1Z 3X1
800-889-2060
www.langevinforest.com
Tools, wood and books

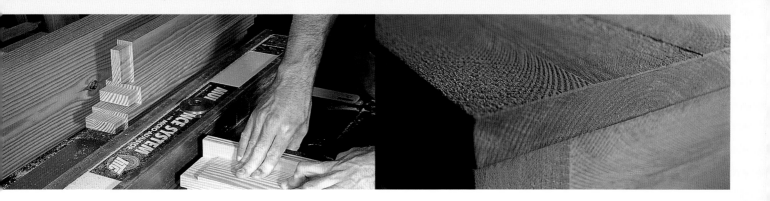

LEE VALLEY TOOLS LTD. & VERITAS TOOLS INC.
U.S.:
P.O. Box 1780
Ogdensburg, New York 13669-6780
800-267-8735
Canada:
P.O. Box 6295, Station J
Ottawa, Ontario
Canada K2A 1T4
800-267-8761
www.leevalley.com
Fine woodworking tools and hardware

LOWE'S HOME IMPROVEMENT CENTER
P.O. Box 1111
North Wilkesboro, North Carolina 28656
800-445-6937
www.lowes.com
Tools, paint, wood, electrical, garden

PAXTON HARDWARE, LTD.
P.O. Box 256
Upper Falls, Maryland 21156
800-241-9741
www.paxtonhardware.com
Antique cabinet and furniture hardware

PORTER-CABLE CORPORATION
4825 Highway 45 North
P.O. Box 2468
Jackson, Tennessee 38302-2468
800-487-8665
www.porter-cable.com
Woodworking tools

RICHELIEU HARDWARE
7900, West Henri-Bourassa
Ville St-Laurent, Quebec
Canada
H4S 1V4
800-619-5446 (U.S.)
800-361-6000 (Canada)
www.richelieu.com
Hardware supplies

ROCKLER WOODWORKING AND HARDWARE
4365 Willow Drive
Medina, Minnesota 55340
800-299-4441
www.rockler.com
Woodworking hardware and supplies

STANLEY HAND TOOLS
480 Myrtle Street
New Britain, Connecticut 06053
860-225-5111
www.stanleytools.com
Hand tools

TOOLSTATION
18 Whiteladies Road
Clifton
Bristol, U.K.
BS8 2LG
0808-100-7-2-11
www.toolstation.com
Power tools

TRIANGLE COATINGS, INC.
1930 Fairway Drive
San Leandro, California 94577
510-614-3900
www.modernoptions.com
Modern Options antiquing solutions

WICKES
Wickes House
120-138 Station Road
Harrow
Middlesex
HA1 2QB
0870 6089001
www.wickes.co.uk
Tools and home woodworking equipment

WOODCRAFT SUPPLY CORP.
P.O. Box 1686
Parkersburg, West Virginia 26102-1686
800-535-4482
www.woodcraft.com
Woodworking hardware and accessories

WOODFINISHINGSUPPLIES.COM
866-548-1677
www.woodfinishingsupplies.com
Valspar Professional Glaze

WOODWORKER'S SUPPLY
1108 North Glenn Road
Casper, Wyoming 82601
800-645-9292
www.woodworker.com
Woodworking tools and accessories; finishing supplies; books and plans

index